COBB COUNTY

COBB COUNTY

At The Heart Of Change

TEXT BY JANE HILL

PHOTOGRAPHS BY FLIP CHALFANT

LONGSTREET PRESS
Atlanta, Georgia

PUBLISHED IN COOPERATION WITH
THE COBB CHAMBER OF COMMERCE

Published by
LONGSTREET PRESS, INC.
2150 Newmarket Parkway
Suite 102
Marietta, Georgia 30067

Printed in Singapore
95 94 93 92 91   5 4 3 2 1

Library of Congress Catalog Card Number: 91-061933

ISBN 1-56352-000-1

This book was printed by Tien Wah Press in Singapore. The text type was set by Coghill Book Typesetting, Richmond, Virginia, and type for corporate profiles was set by Type Designs, Inc., Atlanta, Georgia. Art direction, design, and production by Laura Ellis. Corporate profile sales, book development, and production management by Bookmark.

Cover photo: Overlook Building, Vinings.

CONTENTS

Foreword

To imagine a better place to live and work than Cobb County, Georgia, is practically impossible. Nature and man have joined forces to create something of great beauty, terrific energy, and enviable strength. Cobb County: At the Heart of Change captures, in words and pictures, the story of how Cobb's citizens, past and present, have shaped nature's bounty into the miracle that is present-day Cobb County.

We at the Chamber of Commerce are proud to have been a part of the most exciting and dynamic era in Cobb's history. The years from 1942 to 1992, our fiftieth anniversary, coincide with the county's movement from a quiet rural community to one of the country's most dynamic suburban-urban centers. The Chamber has been a big part of that growth and progress, a role we relish and a commitment that will carry us into the next century.

Cobb County has been called the Small Business Capital of America, and the Chamber serves as the glue that holds the thriving, ever-expanding network of businesses—small and large—together. Farsighted businesspeople seized on Cobb's potential in the late fifties and early sixties and transformed their vision for the area into today's reality, setting the tone and providing a model for today's Chamber.

Like these visionary leaders, today's Chamber is ready to push for those things that will make tomorrow's Cobb everything it can be. When our 1983 survey of businesses revealed that transportation is a major concern, the Chamber established a transportation task force and set in motion plans for funding transportation improvements still in progress today.

When the interests of Lockheed are at stake, the interests of Cobb County are at stake. Thus, the Chamber never ceases its lobbying efforts on behalf of this friendly giant, the county's largest industry.

The Chamber's job doesn't stop at exerting leadership. We also work hard to attract leadership to Cobb. Many businesses and businesspeople who've chosen Cobb County as their headquarters could have located anywhere in the country. But they chose Cobb because we've got a "can-do" atmosphere—an energy for progress and a respect for tradition and values—that's hard to match. People can get things done here that they can't get done elsewhere. It's that simple.

We're pleased to be a part of the hard work that goes into creating that simplicity, that "can-do" atmosphere. We're also pleased to be a part of this book, which makes tangible some of the intangibles that go into making Cobb County the miraculous place it is. The theme at the Cobb Chamber is "Get Caught Up in the Spirit." I can think of no better way for visitors, lifelong residents, and newcomers to do just that than to sit back and enjoy Cobb County: At the Heart of Change.

Welcome to Cobb. We invite you to enjoy and to participate. To join us as we continue the phenomenal story.

—— Phil Sanders, President,
Cobb Chamber of Commerce

As Cobb County, Georgia, prepared to enter the 1990s, its population had reached almost 450,000, making the county larger than incorporated Atlanta. Projections indicate that by the turn of the century Cobb, now third in total population, will have become the state's second-most populous county.

The eighties were a period of tremendous growth in Cobb; in that decade alone population increased 50.4 percent, compared to a national average increase of 9.8 percent and an increase of 18.6 percent in the state of Georgia. The Atlanta Regional Commission put the overall growth rate for the county in the past decade at 48 percent, citing Cobb's ever-expanding, sound economic base and its business leadership's commitment to growth as reasons for the healthy expansion.

Dubbed America's "Small Business Capital," Cobb County supports and courts entrepreneurs and other small businesses through its diversified economy, supportive banking, fertile land, and strong educational resources and business leadership. The result is one of the country's most "user-friendly" business environments.

But another key factor in growth is Cobb's unique blend of metropolitan living in a country setting, its unmistakable and enduring sense of character, which permeates all its towns and neighborhoods. Simply put, Cobb continues to grow because it is a terrific place to live and work.

Nor is Cobb one of those communities whose heyday is past. In fact, just the opposite. In a study commissioned by the *Wall Street Journal*, the Cambridge, Massachusetts firm Cognetics, Inc., named the Marietta-Roswell area the nation's number-one "Boom Town of the 1990s," and the newspaper itself has called the Cobb area one of the nation's top-ten "go-go growth towns." ARC projections call for 51,500 new jobs to be created in Cobb County between 1989-1993, and officials estimate that by 2010 the county will support 406,000 jobs, a 320 percent increase over 1980.

As recently as World War II, 80 percent of Cobb County was farmland; today farms account for less than 1 percent of its land. According to the 1980 census, only 65 percent of Cobb's residents had lived here for more than five years; 20 percent of citizens older than five lived in another state five years earlier. By almost any measure one chooses, Cobb County is truly a community at the heart of change. In the fifty-year history of its Chamber of Commerce, the largest county-wide chamber in the state, Cobb has undergone the most profound sorts of transformation a community can. Yet it has retained much of its past identity— the values, the traditions, the energy and spirit that have defined its character since the early 1830s when white citizens first moved onto land that had, until that time, been the province of the Cherokee nation.

From this blend of rapid progress toward tomorrow and steady adherence to the strengths of yesterday, Cobb County has shaped a dynamic present, perhaps unmatched anywhere and certainly worth the serious attention of anyone considering relocation. Cobb County Commission Chairman Philip Secrist characterizes the county as "suburban in structure . . . cosmopolitan in character," and he credits past leaders with the "foresight and courage" to plan for today's "plentiful, clean water and efficient wastewater treatment, strong protective services, numerous parks and libraries, and an expanding array of health and human services."

This strong infrastructure is re-

inforced by an equally impressive
human presence. The *Atlanta Business Chronicle* says of Cobb's citizens, "Turn virtually any stone in
Cobb County and you'll find an influential person. The movers and
shakers of the metro area seem to
flock north to hold court and oversee
their corporate empires."

Perhaps at no single spot in
Cobb are the castles of those empires
more impressive than in the area that
has come to be known as the "Platinum Triangle." Situated at the intersection of the county's three major
transportation arteries—I-75, I-285,
and U.S. Highway 41—the Triangle
is home to the Cumberland/Galleria
hub of business, shopping, and
cultural riches that first drew national and international attention to
what was once a rural area turned
bedroom community, with a healthy
smattering of Civil War history to
furnish raw material for local yarn-
spinners.

From that natural modern-day
convergence of trade and transportation, Cobb County has spun a story
more amazing than any single epi-
sode in its colorful history. The Platinum Triangle is but one shining
shape in the collage of evolving
Cobb. Anchoring the county at its
southern end, the Triangle now has a
counterpart and rival at the northern
end of Cobb in the Barrett/Town
Center area near the intersection of
I-75 and I-575. This northern area
of Cobb was the best remaining evidence of the county's rural era as
recently as ten years ago. Now it is the
fastest-growing area, one of metropolitan Atlanta's rising-star locations.

This north-south path is as ancient as the inhabited history of the
area. Long before international corporations located along this major
artery, the Cherokees and their
neighbors, the Creeks, trod a
wooded path that was their channel
of commerce and connection. In our
beginnings, we can see ourselves.

The portion of Cherokee land that would eventually become Cobb County consists of rolling foothills, broad ridges, and narrow valleys. It's a topography of transition, where the piedmont meets the mountains. Covered by lush green meadows and wooded hills, the physical landscape of Cobb has always been a thing of beauty. Its soil is primarily the red clay for which its region of the South is noted. The land is particularly fertile along the many creeks and streams that lace the territory. Most of these tributaries flow into the Chattahoochee River, which passes through Cobb on its way to the Gulf of Mexico and forms the boundary between Cobb County and Atlanta, lying to the southeast.

A beautiful landscape and fertile soil are not the only natural assets Cobb County has to offer. The Cherokees and all who have followed them have enjoyed an almost ideal climate: in January, the coldest month, the average temperature is 41.9 degrees Fahrenheit; in July, 78.6. Average annual rainfall is just under forty-nine inches. Winter brings minimal snowfall; in many years, none at all. The mild springs often arrive in early March and linger well into June with a bountiful display of azaleas, dogwoods, and daffodils. Cobb's abundance of trees and its proximity to the North Georgia mountains make autumn perhaps even more beautiful. Autumn too often lingers, sometimes threatening to wait around for Christmas.

Indian groups moved into northwest Georgia at about the same time that English settlers began coming to the coastal region around Savannah. The Creek nation settled in present-day Cobb County in the 1700s. When an 1819 treaty granted the land to the Cherokee nation, the Creeks moved south, back across the

Chattahoochee River into what is now Fulton County.

The Indian villages within Cobb were key trading and negotiating sites, in part because the territory marked the convergence of two major nations: the Creek and the Cherokee. Standing Peachtree, a Creek town on both sides of the Chattahoochee at the mouth to Peachtree Creek, was the place to enter the

Cherokees' land; thus, Standing Peachtree became a center of commerce between the two Indian groups and the early white settlers. U.S. 41, Cobb's main thoroughfare for most of its history, was originally an Indian path called Peachtree Trail. In fact, the Indian trading routes are one of the most significant remnants of their occupation. Whites followed them in developing their own communities and trade routes, upgrading the single-file footpaths to horse trails, then wagon paths. Eventually, these same routes were widened, bridged, and paved.

Another living reminder of the county's Indian citizens is the names they left behind: Kennesaw, Sope Creek, Allatoona, Nickajack. But after the Cherokee Removal of 1838, an act of the federal government ensuring that the Cherokees relinquished all claim to any land in the state of Georgia, the Indian influence on the county's economy, society, geography, and politics effectively ended. The Indians were extraordinary trustees of nature's gifts. They

loved and appreciated the land and dealt with it accordingly. They settled sparsely and lived in peace with nature and its creatures. They left behind an abundance from which their successors have benefited for more than 150 years now.

In the days before the Cherokee removal, the federal government encouraged economic interaction between Indians and settlers. The state of Georgia stressed settlement. Spanish explorer Hernando DeSoto is believed to be the first white man to visit the area, sometime in the early 1500s. The original European settlers came mostly from England, Scotland, or Ireland, with some of Germanic origin as well. They came, at first, primarily in search of gold.

In fact, gold fever led, at least indirectly, to Andrew Jackson's decision to remove the Cherokee from the territory. Once that had been done and the Indians were on their way to Oklahoma along the infamous "Trail of Tears," a lottery was held and winners were awarded portions of the former Indian territory. Cherokee land was divided into forty-acre gold tracts and 160-acre farm tracts. However, most of the gold proved to be farther north, and many of those early settlers who passed through Cobb saw the potential for successful farming.

The combination of fertile land, ample water, and a climate conducive to long growing seasons became almost as irresistible as gold. From the time the county was created, on December 3, 1832, until the opening of the Bell bomber plant in 1943 moved Cobb County into the mainstream of twentieth-century life, the area remained essentially rural, and its economy was primarily agricultural.

The typical farm in the northern region of Georgia was built on a model quite different from the more famous and more often mythologized

plantation model of the coastal region. The farm immigrants' goal was more often subsistence than commerce or culture. Most settlers worked small farms with little or no slave labor. At the outset of the Civil War, slaves made up only 27 percent of Cobb's population, compared to 44 percent statewide. In part, the small farm was necessitated by the Upper Piedmont's terrain. Hilly land made plantations impractical.

But the self-sufficiency that marked the plantation model of agriculture was also a feature of these smaller upcountry farms. Unlike English or European models, where farm houses were closely grouped and fields were scattered outward from the village, or town, the typical upcountry configuration put a house and its accompanying outbuildings in the center of the owner's land, with his fields extending outward, thus separating him from his neighbors.

The holdings of a single landowner often resembled a village in and of themselves. Larger communities were often defined by gristmills, blacksmith's shops, and churches. Most shopping took place in a general store attached to milling and/or blacksmith services. Inns, so typical of an English rural setting, were rare in Cobb's early days.

The earliest settlers weren't necessarily interested in perma-

nence. Since sawmills and railroads quickly followed the original white settlers, frame houses were common from the beginning. Even so, mobility was crucial—the farmers planned to move on when soil was exhausted. Thus, they needed sturdy, functional homes, but cared little for decorative frills. Rails, split and stacked, served as fences instead of the more permanent stone and rock walls common in New England and, before that, in Europe.

The earliest efforts to organize the scattered farms and families into some community structure took the form of militia districts. A group of one hundred households could band together and petition to be a militia district, a defensive group, expected to protect against outside threats. Perhaps the concept of the militia district lives on in more than voting precincts and school districts. Neighbors banding together to provide for the mutual defense of home and hearth in today's Cobb call their efforts neighborhood-watch programs.

Like Indian names, the early settlers' perceptions of their environment live on in many of the county's place names: Rottenwood, Mud, and Sweetwater creeks, and Brushy and Pine mountains are examples. Other names honor the first settlers and developers: Howell, Pace, Johnson, McLain. The county itself is named for Thomas W. Cobb, a former U.S. Senator and a well-respected and admired judge. Cobb himself never lived in the county, but he was widely known and revered. Marietta is believed to have taken its name from the diminutive of his wife's name, Mary.

Because the county's origins coincide with a transportation boom in the United States—an era of almost frenzied building of canals, railroads, and turnpikes—even Cobb's rural years saw industry and de-velopment become a way of life. But early industry and transportation developments were intended to serve agricultural interests, not redirect the county's economy. By 1849 the county was home to more than twenty gristmills and an equal number of sawmills. Along the creeks, good sources of water power, some merchant mills had also sprung up. But factory development prior to the Civil War never came close to dominating the economy, always re-mained local in scope, and never employed more than a few hundred workers at a given time.

The seeds of Cobb's strong commercial economy lie primarily in the transportation boom that brought the railroad to Cobb. The State of Georgia constructed the Western and Atlantic line from Atlanta to Chattanooga; four of Cobb's six incorporated towns lie along its tracks: Smyrna, Marietta, Kennesaw, and Acworth. The two other incorporated

towns, Powder Springs and Austell, are located along the path of later railroad development. Thus, just as transportation—convenient access to Atlanta's Hartsfield International Airport and the major corridors of I-75 and I-285—has been crucial to the contemporary boom, so too was transportation the key to Cobb's earliest moves away from the rural to the suburban and urban.

The earliest suburbs, in fact, evolved along rail and trolley lines.

By 1905 Marietta was linked to Atlanta by the Atlanta-Marietta Interurban Railway, which crossed an essentially rural landscape to connect two cities. At the time this rail system was the largest of its kind in the Southeast. Each stop along its path generated residential development. Because it remained in operation until just after World War II, its contribution to the land-use patterns within the county are still much in evidence.

Businessmen and professionals dominated the early social and economic life of the county. The Western and Atlantic line encouraged mercantile establishments and small industries, such as tanneries and cotton, wool, and paper mills. The railway also boosted the economy by making Cobb a tourist destination, especially for lowcountry citizens fleeing the threat of yellow fever and other epidemics common to their more tropical climate.

In many ways the definitive business for a nineteenth-century entrepreneur might have been a hotel located along the railroad line in Cobb County. Those who established such enterprises promoted the area's climate and the reputed therapeutic value of the local spring water. Marietta, in particular, became a haven for South Georgia planters escaping the heat and malarial swamps. The tourist market was, ironically, enhanced by the Civil War. After defeating the Confederacy and destroying much of Cobb County during Sherman's march to Atlanta, northerners began to "winter" in Cobb County, using it as a retreat from their own difficult climate, just as the lowcountry planters had been doing for years before the war.

The Civil War, or the War Between the States or, as some locals still prefer, the War of Northern Aggression or the Late Unpleasantness—whatever name it goes by, the war changed Cobb County forever. Its heritage of pre-war buildings and other landmarks was greatly diminished when three of the eight major battles of the march on Atlanta were fought in Cobb County. The county itself became a strategic target because of its factories and railroads, and the Confederacy saw it as a natural area for defensive fighting because of its mountains and the Chattahoochee.

The post-war recovery and reconstruction of factories was largely a private enterprise. The federal government did rebuild the railroads fairly quickly because they were necessary to supplying the occupying forces. That rebuilding also brought thousands of homeless Georgians access to Atlanta and Cobb County, creating enormous strains on the health and welfare systems of both, but also sowing the seeds of the area's eventual booms in population and economy.

The war caused a decrease in land and property values and delayed industrial development. Cotton became the new focus of the county's agricultural enterprises. Large farms were broken down into smaller ones, a retreat to the original agricultural structure of the white settlers.

Twenty-one manufacturing establishments were operating in Cobb by 1870, the first year in the county's history that the value of manufactured goods surpassed that of agricultural goods ($846,000 to $811,000). Thus, even though Cobb remained a predominantly rural community until the advent of World War II, the seeds for its transition lie in the recovery period from an earlier war. By 1940, the eve of the Second World War, the balance between manufactured goods and agricultural goods in Cobb was almost two-to-one in favor of manufacturing: six million dollars to just under three million.

By 1888 Marietta's economy had recovered sufficiently to justify the opening of the Marietta Bank. The Anderson Brothers' store (which later became DuPre's, still in business today) had opened to serve consumers' mercantile needs. Prosperity eventually allowed both the Methodists and the Baptists to build large new sanctuaries. The chief instruments in the recovery were a paper mill, two chair companies, two marble companies, a textile mill, and a machine works.

By 1889 Marietta had electric street lights; sewerage was available in 1896; 1898 brought the first telephones to the city. But many of these signs of prosperity and modern life didn't reach rural Cobb till the mid-twentieth century although some communities saw them sooner through rural improvement programs sponsored by the federal government during the Depression. In general, the post-Civil War years were not easy for rural citizens. Fifty-six percent of the county's farmers in 1900 were tenants rather than landowners; tenants paid one-third of their corn crop and one-quarter of their cotton crop in rent. This lack of economic opportunity kept the county's population low, but it also set the stage for the unbelievable boom years World War II created.

In the early days of the twentieth century, utility interests established a strong presence in Cobb County, which became a major center for gas line connections in north-

and the many smaller ponds utility development created. Once the bodies of water existed for their purposes relating to energy and power, developers began to wonder if they couldn't also serve recreational purposes. Thus, they began to experiment with the concept of small weekend cottages built to encircle these man-made lakes and ponds. The World War II boom meant that Cobb quickly became too urban to serve as a "country getaway" locale, but the concept lives on in a number of Cobb subdivisions that feature small lakes and ponds.

rival Candler Field (now Hartsfield International Airport) in Atlanta. The site was named Rickenbacker Field, to honor the World War I flying ace, and construction by the Army Corps of Engineers took place in 1941 and 1942. In 1943 the newly constructed facility was leased to the Bell Aircraft Company for assembly of B-29 bombers.

And life in Cobb County was forever changed. Twenty-nine thousand workers suddenly converged on Marietta, a city of less than ten thousand. Clearly, the city itself couldn't staff Marietta's first major national industry. Those living in the depressed rural areas, still not fully recovered from the Civil War's blows to the land and the economy and more recently damaged by the Depression, moved to Marietta to work in the factory. Their arrival created a temporary housing crisis that became an ongoing housing boom.

Although the Bell plant closed in 1946, most of those who had moved to town stayed. Their decision paid off. In only five years Lockheed began operations in the same facility to serve Korean War demands for equipment, and Lockheed remains the county's, in fact the state's, largest single manufacturing employer.

Prior to the 1940s Cobb's largest building was probably no taller than four stories and no wider or deeper than half a city block. Today, the buildings of the Platinum Triangle stand tall enough that those on their top floors can see well past Lockheed on a clear day, can see all the way to Barrett, where tomorrow's gleaming towers rise before their eyes. Just as these developments seem to anchor the county's present, so do the Civil War and World War II seem to bracket its history, demonstrating the uncanny way in which loss and suffering can be transformed into beauty and success.

western Georgia. Beginning about 1910, for three decades the electrical power industry brought equal interest and development. Lake Allatoona and Lake Acworth are by-products of this utility interest; the consequent by-product from the lakes was a resurgence and expansion of the tourism trade that was, again, a trademark of the county's early pre-war economy.

Another way in which utility development shaped the current face of the county is in the configuration of neighborhoods around the lakes

Cobb County had about fifty miles of paved roads in 1934, but almost no additional paving went on until after the Second World War. This delay in massive road-paving projects is one reason for the extended rural feel of life in the county.

All that began to change, however, in 1941, not as a result of efforts to improve auto transportation, but because Cobb took its first serious steps into the aviation era. In that year the county purchased six hundred acres of land with the goal of building a municipal airport to

HELEN VANDERHORST

In 1919, when I was eight years old, my family was living in Atlanta. My grandmother died that year, and my grandfather loved his house in Marietta so much that he couldn't bear to leave it even though he wasn't able to live there alone. So we moved to Marietta to live with him.

And that is where I live today, at 267 Whitlock Avenue in Marietta, in a house my grandparents built after my great-grandparents' house, on the same site, was burned during the War Between the States.

I lived here until 1940 when I married and moved with my husband, an Episcopal priest, to Baltimore, Maryland. We eventually lived in Macon, Philadelphia, Chattanooga, and Nashville as well. But when he retired in 1977, the first and only place we thought about living was Marietta. Our friends from other places told me moving back would be a mistake because the place and the people wouldn't be the same.

But I didn't listen. We moved right back to this house, where I grew up, and fitting in was as easy as could be. The very first week I went to my sister's garden club, and all but two of the women there were my old friends. I had been away for almost forty years, but I felt like I had never left.

I love Marietta. I'll never live anywhere else. Not that I think things will never change—I know they are talking about widening my street, Whitlock Avenue, which will mean twice as much traffic going twice as fast. I don't know if my old house can stand all that vibration. But even if they make the street four times wider than it is now, I'll certainly stay right here. This is my home.

Helen VanderHorst has spent most of her life in Marietta.

B y the mid-sixties a new breed of community leader emerged in Cobb County: members of the Kennesaw Mountain Jaycees, including Fred Bentley, Ernest Barrett, Bill Bullard, Romeo Hudgins, and Wyman Pilcher. The county's political establishment quickly dubbed them the "young turks," for the goal of the group was nothing short of radical in the eyes of the establishment.

For starters, the group wanted to change the structure of the county government, which was then a one-man commission. In 1964 the state's General Assembly created a five-member commission, and the young turks persuaded Ernest Barrett to run for commission chairman. He won and held the position for twenty years. Most observers credit Barrett with being the single most influential figure in Cobb's rapid progress and phenomenal growth. During his tenure as chairman, he created a stable environment that business people could trust, persuaded citizens that investing in improved streets and utilities was the key to growth, and worked to lessen the gap between rural Cobb and its more modern, prosperous suburbs by expanding sewers, schools, and parks into the rural areas.

For the young turks, the shifts in Cobb's lifestyle and economy brought about by the Bell and Lockheed plants were only the foreshadowing of what could be an even more remarkable transformation. They wanted to develop Cobb's fullest potential; they weren't content to rest on the laurels of the wartime booms that had brought the possibility of change to the forefront. They had carefully observed the growth and development in nearby DeKalb County during the fifties, and they believed similar change could be beneficial to Cobb. They remembered that many Bell Aircraft

executives chose to remain in Cobb County when their Marietta plant closed. Georgia seemed more appealing than a return to Bell's home in Buffalo, New York. If Bell executives had chosen the benefits of the Cobb life, why couldn't those benefits be used to recruit businesses to the county? And if the urban-suburban mix of higher wages and more complete services had enhanced the lives of farm residents who came seeking a better life, wouldn't the county be doing its citizens a favor to expand the growth of industry and other businesses to give more people that same chance?

As the sixties unfolded and the young turks moved forward, making their vision a reality, transportation. once again emerged to provide a crucial boost to the economy and development of the area. In the early seventies, I-285 through Cobb County was completed, and I-75 was extended north across the Chattahoochee. At the place they met, Cumberland Mall was built, on a site once home to the Boy Scouts' Camp Burt Adams. And the model for Cobb's future development was complete. Cumberland, and later the Galleria complex and the rest of the business / shopping / entertainment complex that is the Platinum Triangle, is an early embodiment of the trend toward "employment nodes" or "urban villages," which are, in turn, a return to an earlier way of organizing our lives around a central location that serves almost every imaginable need.

A wonderful symmetry has emerged in that the fastest-growing part of Cobb today is the northwest portion of the county, where almost six thousand jobs were added to the economy in the late eighties and where the population from 1985 to 1989 grew by more than seven thousand per year. At the intersection of I-75 and I-575 sits Town Center, one

of the region's largest shopping malls. The major thoroughfare in the area is the Ernest Barrett Parkway. It takes riders from Town Center west to the Barrett development that grows daily between I-575 and U.S.

41, a couple of miles to the west. Although Ernest Barrett has died and a new generation of young turks shapes the future, his legacy lives on: the hottest spot in Cobb for business, housing, shopping, and other development was pastureland a decade ago. But Barrett sensed the potential years earlier. It is fitting that a piece of the prosperity he envisioned bear his name.

Cobb County sits north of Atlanta along the Chattahoochee River. It extends north to Lake Allatoona and south to just beyond I-20. Part of the region known as north central Georgia, it is bounded on the north by Cherokee County; the east,

Fulton; the south, Douglas; and the west, Paulding. Today, more than 450,000 people live within these boundaries. Of those, 22 percent live in one of the six incorporated communities: Marietta, Acworth, Austell, Kennesaw, Powder Springs, or Smyrna. The other 78 percent live in unincorporated Cobb, a split that reflects the upcountry farm model from the earliest days of settlement in that organized "villages" have never been the predominant lifestyle here.

This is not, however, to suggest that today's unincorporated Cobb looks or feels like the old days. In fact, without signs, it is often next to impossible to tell where city limits end and unincorporated areas begin. One thing is for sure—little of unincorporated Cobb could be called rural; almost none, farmland.

Marietta is the largest of the six incorporated communities and also the seat of the county government. It is, in fact, the third-largest incorporated community in all of metropolitan Atlanta. Created by an act of the state legislature on December 19,

1834, Marietta prospered quickly as a result of the building of the Western and Atlantic line. Not only did the railroad bring jobs and opportunities to the town, but it also meant that almost from its inception Marietta was connected to national commercial centers.

The site of the original settlement was chosen, according to early records, because it "seemed to be a particularly healthy place," thanks to its easy access to the natural springs near the present-day square. As early as 1840 Marietta was described as "one of the most pleasant towns in Cherokee Georgia," and the completion of the railroad to Chattanooga only increased the town's sophistication. Soirees, traveling shows, and exhibitions became commonplace, and by the 1850s Marietta was experiencing something of a heyday. Summer and permanent residents enjoyed almost daily diversions, including balls, concerts, picnics, and suppers.

The outbreak of the Civil War, of course, changed that atmosphere. The railroad that had brought prosperity suddenly made the town a strategic target for the enemy. Training of cadets at the Georgia Military Institute, less than a mile from the square, suddenly took on new significance, for the cadets and the citizens.

The Kennesaw House sheltered Confederate military operations and the Union spies who planned and executed the famous raid on *The General* up the tracks in Kennesaw. General Sherman also stayed at the Kennesaw House as he passed through Marietta on his march to Atlanta. He burned the hotel and the courthouse in 1864. The hotel was rebuilt as a three- instead of a four-story structure after the war, giving rise to rumors of haunting. Legend has it that the failure to rebuild the fourth floor left hundreds of restless spirits to wander the newly constructed lower levels.

Spirits linger in a more solemn way as well. The National Cemetery, established as a result of the war, is home to the graves of ten thousand Union soldiers. In 1866 and 1867 Henry Cole, a Mariettan loyal to the

Union, donated a parcel of land between Washington Avenue and Roswell Street, in hopes that a joint Union-Confederate cemetery would help heal ill feelings that lingered. That plan failed, however, and the U.S. government accepted his gift for a national military cemetery. In addition to the Union soldiers who rest there, victims of six subsequent wars, including the Persian Gulf War, are buried in the Marietta cemetery. Ceremonies to honor the dead are held each year on Veterans and Memorial days.

Not far away is the Confederate Cemetery, which began with the burial of a single soldier, W. H. Miller, M.D., in early September 1863. This cemetery's early growth and development were due largely to the efforts of three Marietta women— Catherine Winn, Ann Moyer, and Jane Glover, who donated the land. The numbers of dead laid to rest here greatly increased during the battle at Kennesaw Mountain. Eventually the cemetery became the final resting place for approximately three thousand men from fourteen states. Each year on the Sunday closest to Confederate Memorial Day (April 26) a commemorative service is held.

Tourism helped Marietta to recover from the war more quickly than some southern towns. Its traditional visitors from the Georgia coast were joined by northerners coming to see for themselves the place described by soldiers lucky enough to have made it home.

The railroad was also rebuilt fairly quickly so that reconstructionists could be easily supported and supplied. By 1870 activity around the square was prosperous enough to require its being refenced to keep animals away. In an 1887 Western and Atlantic pamphlet, Joseph M. Brown, later to be governor of Georgia, described Marietta

as "one of the prettiest little cities in all the Southland. . . . It well deserves the title of 'The Little Gem City of Georgia!'"

A variety of industrial plants had established themselves within the city by 1900, and the gap between the prosperous city and its less thriving rural neighbors began to widen, a pattern that would continue up until the advent of the Bell plant in the forties, when the rural neighbors moved to the city to carve their own slice of prosperity.

Marietta is still known as the Gem City of the South, and although its growth slowed considerably in the early eighties, it remains the county's largest city. And despite Sherman's devastation, a surprising number of historic homes and buildings remain, enough to support five designated historic districts and a walking tour, sponsored by the Marietta Welcome Center, featuring fifty-two homes and public buildings. Within the city limits

visitors can find at least one hundred pre-twentieth-century homes, many clustered along Church and Cherokee streets and Kennesaw Avenue and the streets running off these major arteries.

Among the Atlanta area's first bed-and-breakfast establishments was Marietta's Marlow House. Its current function is, like many things in Cobb, true to its historical roots. Built in 1887 by Miss Idele Marlow, the house was not only her residence but also a respectable means of earning an independent income for its single owner. Through such "respectable" means, many women entered the economy of Cobb in the early days, and they continue to play a major role today, having broadened considerably the spectrum of respectable work.

Just down Church Street from the Marlow House is another home that now operates as a bed-and-breakfast establishment but that also reflects an important piece of the county's history. The Stanley House, a four-story Queen Anne structure with thirteen-foot ceilings, was built in 1895 as a summer home—part of the tourist industry that helped young Marietta to prosper. Its original owner was Felie Woodrow of Columbia, South Carolina; her nephew, Woodrow Wilson, became president of the United States.

The Marietta Welcome Center, established in 1984 as part of the city's sesquicentennial celebration, hosts twenty thousand visitors each year. Located in the old Western and Atlantic station built in 1898, the Welcome Center offers visitors historic film and slide presentations, walking tours, historic exhibits, and current information on both Marietta and Cobb County.

The Center shares office space with the Downtown Marietta Development Authority, which the state legislature established in 1975 to encourage renovation of the historic areas around the square. The goal was to recapture the look of the late nineteenth and early twentieth centuries and to make the square once again the focal point of community life, as it was during its pre- and post-Civil War heydays.

During the seventies Representative Howard "Red" Atherton planted the seeds that led to efforts to revitalize the town square. Renovation of Glover Park, as the square is named, for a prominent family of Marietta's early years, was completed in 1986. John Williams, founder of Post Properties, gave the project its biggest boost with a quarter-million-dollar donation. Jack Wilson provided significant leadership; Harold Willingham do-

nated the fountain. In May 1986 a dedication ceremony took place, and the community was invited to observe what the efforts of many, including the in-kind services of several city departments, had wrought.

Brick walkways, built by the city's schoolchildren, who each gave a dollar, connect landscaped gardens, a sculptured fountain, and a gazebo with a copper roof and a weathervane. The gazebo instantly became a popular spot for weddings; visitors will witness at least one ceremony on almost any weekend during spring, summer, and fall. The park also features a stage equipped with a professional sound system, scene of free concerts during the summer and community meetings and other events year-round. There's also a children's play area, complete with a replica of *The General*. The Victorian charm is tangible, down to the delicate wrought-iron fence that surrounds the entire square.

But Glover Park is not just pretty to look at. The Development Authority's goal of making the square once again the center of community life has been realized. In addition to the summer concert series, the park is host to a number of annual events: craft shows in spring and fall, an old-fashioned 4th of July

celebration, complete with fireworks, an Art in the Park display by local artists, and a pilgrimage tour of homes in December that begins and ends in the park.

A revitalized park has also meant revitalized shopping and entertainment. Without walking more than a city block or two, you can dine on French, Greek, southern, and classic American cuisine. The best hot dogs in Cobb are here, as is some of America's best antique shopping. You can buy books, fine art, clothing, and all manner of tricks, disguises, and magic. An active and critically acclaimed theater and romantic horse-and-buggy rides round out the picture.

Not far from the square, at the intersection of Roswell Street and U.S. 41, stands the modern counterpoint to the turn-of-the-century romance of Glover Park: the Big Chicken, a landmark so famous and so dominant that pilots navigate by it and the writers of television's *Designing Women* refer to it to give their scripts authenticity. Designed by a Georgia Tech student and built in 1963, the Big Chicken is truly *big*: a fifty-six-foot triangular metal rooster, standing guard over a fried-chicken restaurant. Originally, his eyes rolled, his beak opened and shut, his comb dipped in the breeze. Al-

though the design dealt with the possibility of hundred-mile-per-hour winds, when the motor to activate the Chicken's "features" was first turned on, all the windows in the restaurant shattered. Thus, the active features were abandoned in the interest of safety and windows. The Big Chicken is perhaps the only fowl ever to have been honored by his own art show, the Grand Poulet exhibit, in which local artists offered amazingly varied interpretations of the bird.

Newcomers are almost always puzzled by the immediate response to any query about directions in Cobb County. Natives begin their explanation by saying, "Do you know where the Big Chicken is?" If the answer is yes, you can get anywhere from there. If it's no, you have to find out before you can navigate Cobb—and before you'll be able to give directions yourself.

Marietta has two sister cities in conjunction with the Sister Cities International program. Beginning in 1969 Marietta established a relationship with the German city of Linz. In Linz there's a Marietta Street, and near the square Marietta has a Linz-am-Rhein Walk. The special fondness that Linz's citizens feel for Marietta stems from the efforts of Mariettan Dewey Holmes, who helped rebuild Linz after World War II. The other sister city is Heredia in Costa Rica.

An analysis done at the end of the eighties by the *Atlanta Journal and Constitution*, which considered property tax rates, level of services, available housing, utilities, and schools, concluded that Marietta was the best place to live in the nine-county metropolitan area. It is the only place with a Big Chicken.

Acworth, sometimes called the Lake City, because of its proximity to lakes Allatoona and Acworth, lies north of Marietta in the fast-growing northwestern sector of the county. It is, in fact, the northernmost of the incorporated communities.

The 325 acres of Lake Acworth and Acworth Beach, only minutes from the city's Main Street, are the focal point of community activity. Only a thin strip of land separates the smaller lake from twelve-thousand-acre Lake Allatoona, so water sports and other recreational opportunities are abundant.

The rapid growth Acworth experienced during the eighties has led to plans for a direct connection between the city and I-75 and to an improved traffic flow for Main Street. Plans also call for additional parking to provide easier access to the abun-

dance of small shops and other retail outlets in the downtown area.

The Western and Atlantic arrived in what is now Acworth in 1842. In 1843 the settlement was named Northcutt Station, after the first station master, Alfred Northcutt. Later that year Lewis Gregg, a W&A surveyor, renamed it Acworth, after his hometown in New Hampshire. Acworth means "oak farm."

A post office opened in 1845, and in 1860, just months before the outbreak of the Civil War, the city was incorporated by the General Assembly. Sherman's march destroyed most of the newly formed town, but he left the Methodist Church standing, reportedly because the soldiers didn't want to disturb a Masonic group that met in its attic.

A Coats & Clark factory, the town's oldest, remains important to

Acworth's economic base. Since the war lumber, hosiery, and tapestry factories have also made Acworth home.

Because of its proximity to the lakes and the mountains and because it is still not directly linked to the interstate, Acworth retains a charm and peacefulness that recalls yesterday more vividly than some other parts of the county. But the community is also poised on the edge of tremendous growth potential, making the nineties an exciting time for the Lake City. And Acworth is ready, already planning for the challenges ahead, at the same time its citizens treasure the tranquility and pleasure their setting provides.

At the other end of the county, in its southwest corner, sits Austell, which was incorporated on September 4, 1885, and named for Alfred Austell, founder of the Atlanta National Bank and builder of Atlanta's Austell Building, now home to the *Atlanta Journal and Constitution*. As a financier Austell played an important role in Georgia's early development; he also once owned a ferry that crossed the Chattahoochee between South Fulton and Douglas counties, not far from the community that bears his name.

The current city of Austell lies on or near the site of the southernmost Cherokee settlement, called Sweetwater Creek during its Indian days. The Cherokees were the first to discover the medicinal properties of the nearby springs that were to help Austell prosper as a tourist destination in the early days. First called Causey's Chapel for an early settler family, the town was later called Irvine, or Irvineville, to honor A. H. Irvine, who built the first known store and served as postmaster. Austell does not lie along the original Western and Atlantic rail line, but in 1880 a line from Atlanta came through what is now Austell. From

there, one branch went to Birmingham, Alabama; another, to Cincinnati, Ohio. Thus, in the early 1880s the settlement was called Cincinnati Junction.

Once the railroad reached the town, it quickly became a popular resort. The Sweetwater Park Hotel boasted four hundred rooms and fifteen landscaped acres during its heyday in the 1880s. The town's life continued to revolve around the tourist trade until after World War I. The popular mineral water from nearby Bowden Lithia Springs is still bottled, but little other physical evidence of the numerous resorts of the early 1900s now exists.

Another important early business, and one of the most long-lived in the county, was the Perkerson family's cornmeal mill on Sweetwater Creek; it operated from 1851 until 1963. Burned by Sherman in 1864, the mill was rebuilt and remained in the Perkerson family until 1963, when it was sold to Martha White and then to Beatrice Foods. The operation was closed and the facilities torn down in 1982 and 1983.

Austell also had the first public school in the county, a predecessor of the current Austell Elementary. In 1990 the school celebrated its one-hundredth anniversary.

In 1987 the town remodeled the old Austell Gas Company building into a new city hall. This refurbishing is another reminder of the important role utilities have played in the county's development. The city-owned gas system adds more than a half-million dollars per year to Austell's revenues. Part of a thriving South Cobb alliance for the arts and development, Austell stands ready to benefit from the hard work those groups have done in the eighties.

Kennesaw, the Cobb community most visited by Civil War buffs, made national headlines in 1982 when the town passed an ordi-

nance requiring all heads of households to own a firearm. First conceived in response to an Illinois town's ban on guns, the ordinance has never been actively enforced, and no gun shop operates within the city limits. Conscientious objectors and convicted felons are exempt from the requirement.

But the spirit of independence and, some would say, feistiness demonstrated by Kennesaw's gun ordinance is the connecting thread in its history as a community.

On April 12, 1862, *The General*, a Western and Atlantic train, stopped for breakfast in Big Shanty, the original name of present-day Kennesaw. On board were John Andrews and twenty Union spies, who came to be known as Andrews's Raiders. They had hatched a plan to

hijack the train while staying at the Kennesaw House in Marietta. Their ultimate goal was to use the commandeered train to burn all bridges between Atlanta and Chattanooga in an effort to seal Atlanta off from all supplies and reinforcements.

While the other passengers dined at the Lacey Hotel, Andrews and his raiders set their plan in motion. They stole *The General* and headed north toward Chattanooga with several cars still attached to the engine when they departed.

General conductor William A. Fuller and his crew pursued the thieves, commandeering a handcar and several engines themselves. At one point in the chase, which is the subject of the Disney movie *The Great Locomotive Chase*, they used a southbound engine, *The Texas*, moving in reverse to continue their pursuit.

Andrews's plan failed when *The General* ran out of steam after eight hours and eighty-seven miles. The hijackers damaged neither the tracks nor the Confederate supply lines. Andrews and seven others were hanged. Some of his conspirators escaped; six were eventually recaptured and later exchanged for southern prisoners. These six ultimately became the first recipients of the newly created Congressional Medal of Honor—an award that, like their plan, was conceived in Marietta's Kennesaw House.

Today, *The General* is the focal point of Kennesaw's Big Shanty museum. The train's retrieval is another adventure story, told in its entirety at the museum and relished by numerous visitors each year.

A more solemn reminder of Kennesaw's history is the Kennesaw Mountain National Battlefield Park.

The mountain figured prominently in the Atlanta campaign of 1864. General Johnston's fifty thousand Confederate troops fortified themselves behind it as Sherman's almost 100,000 Union troops advanced. Frustrated by a month of rain that made going over roads around the mountain impossible, impatient Union forces chose to attack and suffered a stunning defeat. Of course, the rains eventually ended, and the Confederates were forced to abandon their stronghold. The siege and fall of Atlanta soon followed.

Thousands of visitors each year enjoy hiking trails and picnic spots as they mingle with abandoned cannons and deserted earthworks, lasting reminders of the lives lost, on both sides, on these slopes.

In downtown Kennesaw, businessman and Confederacy buff Dent Myers, proprietor of Wild Man's, one of the area's largest collections of war memorabilia, offers his own brand of war reminiscence. A colorful character, Myers also became something of a national celebrity as a spokesperson for the town during the 1982 gun ordinance fame.

Kennesaw's story, however, does not begin with the Civil War. Like most of Cobb's incorporated communities, Kennesaw's history is linked to the railroad and to medicinal springs. High ground and abundant water are, in fact, the chief determining factors in the settlement's original site.

Before the white man arrived, both the Creek and the Cherokee visited the spring located behind the current city hall. The Cherokees called it "Equa Ganugo Gr Ama," which translates "The Big Spring of Water." Because the spring is located near the Creek-Cherokee border, it was a long-standing meeting place for the two tribes until the state of Georgia took over all Indian territory.

In 1838 a haphazard construction camp for sheltering and feeding railroad workers was built near the spring. Originally called Big Grade, it soon became Big Shanty, a name that lives on in a school, a street, businesses, and other features of contemporary life in Kennesaw. The town was virtually destroyed by Sherman, but the citizens rebuilt and incorporated as the town of Kennesaw in 1887, taking their name from the nearby mountain.

Several homes from the 1800s have been restored. Some remain residences; others house businesses. In 1976 the Kennesaw Town Council used a Bicentennial Grant to restore the spring to its original clean, wholesome state. The result, a rock-enclosed area behind city hall, is one of the town's prettiest, most peaceful spots.

Although its downtown looks much as it has for many years, the larger area known as Kennesaw is the county's fastest-growing community, rapidly evolving into a sprawling, prosperous commercial and retail development zone with accompanying upscale housing and entertainment: quite a transition for a settlement that began as a shanty town for Irish railroad men.

A settlement of log houses clustered around mineral springs in 1819 was the beginning of the Powder Springs community, one of Cobb's oldest. Soon the small settlement became a center for commerce. In 1838 its first sawmill opened, and the farmers who made up most of the population were known for clearing the public cow pasture once a week for a baseball game. In 1839 the first frame house was erected, and the community incorporated under the name Springville, in honor of the waters that were the center of community life.

Tourists once flocked to the tiny

settlement, whose mineral-laden springs were famous for turning the surrounding sand gunpowder black; hence, the name Powder Springs. The image of the gunpowder-like sand was strong enough that when the original city charter was repealed in 1850 and efforts to reincorporate succeeded in 1859,

Although the town was occupied during the Civil War, no battles were fought there. The oldest remaining home in Powder Springs, The Ivies, was built in 1866. In 1882 the railroad connected Powder Springs with other areas, and in its agricultural heyday the town's farmers shipped eight hundred bales of

farmers to lower their prices dramatically in an eventually successful effort to drive Georgians out of the cheese business.

Powder Springs had its own Domestic Electric Company long before Georgia Power existed. In 1908 the 7th District Agricultural and Mechanical School opened its doors on

citizens chose to rename their community what many had called it all along. Since then, the town has been known as Powder Springs. The older name, Springville, lives on in the Springville Lodge Number 153 of Free and Accepted Masons, which was founded and named in 1848, before the repeal of the original charter.

cotton per year to Atlanta by train. When cotton failed as a cash crop, farmers formed a cooperative and established a cheese factory with the assistance of the Georgia Agricultural Extension Service. Participating farmers and their wives, who often did more of the cheese-related work, were successful enough to force Wisconsin cheese

208 acres just outside the town. When the state closed the A&M school, the grounds became a public high school. In 1948 John McEachern's widow left 80 percent of her personal stock in trust for the school, which was renamed for her husband. McEachern High is the state's only privately endowed public high school, a fact that reflects the central role of churches and schools in Powder Springs.

Sarah Frances Miller, a Powder Springs native who has lived on its main street since 1920, recalls that "Marietta Street used to be a dirt road lined with oak trees. Those trees were so big they used to meet in the middle over the street." Progress felled the trees she remembers, except those in front of Emma Camp's house. She sat on her porch with a shotgun to protect them.

The spirit of Emma Camp's preservation efforts lives on in the rapidly growing community. The town's population has increased 97 percent in the past decade, but residents are working to preserve the small-town atmosphere while they improve the quality of life and take advantage of the opportunities presented by their booming growth.

In 1978 the Powder Springs Industrial Development Authority was organized to encourage and shape business development. One result has been the establishment of two industrial parks with a thousand undeveloped acres zoned for industrial and commercial use. In 1987 the town invested seven million dollars in refurbishing its square: a fountain, lots of green grass with benches, period street lights, and expansive landscaping blend with the city hall and a growing array of retail establishments. Not far from the redone square, the original springs still pump the water said to contain twenty-six minerals.

Active groups in Powder Springs include youth programs, civic associations, the historical society, a gardening club, and the Governor's Community of Pride Commit-

tee, whose goal is making sure the best of yesterday and tomorrow are integral to what happens in today's Powder Springs.

First known as Ruff's Siding and then as Varner's Station, Smyrna takes its name from one of the Apostle Paul's churches in what is modern-day Turkey. Smyrna is the name given to the nondenominational religious campground that eventually became the center of the settlement's social and religious life after its establishment in 1832 as the scene of grape-arbor meetings.

During railroad construction from 1836 to 1842 Smyrna began the shift from rural village to booming community. Its first brick building, the Smyrna Institute, an academy for boys, was erected in 1850. After Sherman passed through the town, this was the only downtown building left standing. It is now used as a Masonic lodge.

In 1872 the city incorporated; the first elections were held in 1873. Eighteen seventy-two is also the year the Concord Covered Bridge was built just west of Smyrna. It replaced a bridge (circa 1840) destroyed during the Civil War. Citizens Daniell and Ruff, owners of nearby land and mills, constructed the covered bridge, of Queensport design. It is the only covered bridge still in use on public highways in metropolitan

Atlanta. At the turn of the century, the trolley line from Atlanta to Marietta made Smyrna one of Atlanta's first suburban communities.

Modern Smyrna can claim several distinctions. In 1946 the town elected Lorena Pace Pruitt mayor, one of the first women in the country to hold such office. In the mid-1950s the Belmont Hills Shopping Center was completed; at the time it was the Southeast's largest.

Called the Jonquil City in honor of that flower's proliferation during spring, Smyrna received the City Innovation Achievement Award from the Georgia Municipal Association in 1990. The award was for the community center and library complex being constructed as part of an extensive plan to revitalize the downtown area. Fifty-one parcels of land were acquired in order to rebuild in "old" Smyrna.

The first fifteen-million-dollar phase of the project, financed through the Smyrna Downtown Development Authority, includes a fifty-five-thousand-square-foot community center, which will include

gymnasiums, meeting rooms, administrative areas, and athletic facilities. The design is aimed toward the creation of a central gathering place in addition to making a home for the parks and recreation department. The community center will be the first building to occupy a village green that will eventually connect it and the planned city hall, fire and police departments, and library. The green will be the focal point for events such as the annual Jonquil Festival. The master plan also includes space for retail outlets, restaurants, and upscale housing.

Smyrna is the second-largest of Cobb's incorporated communities and home to its largest industrial park, Highlands Industrial Park, and twenty shopping centers and plazas. Stung by a July 1988 *National Geographic* article that labeled it a "redneck" town, Smyrna is ready to prove that it isn't at all. It sees itself as an "urban community with a hometown flavor," a family-oriented town committed to progress and to the spirit of its roots as a vibrant social center.

TREY MOORES

When I first came to Cobb County, I had lived most of my life in Tennessee, and I was very set in my ways. I dreaded my family's move. Once I started classes at Marietta Junior High, at the beginning of my sixth-grade year, I became even more discontent. I actually feigned sickness on several occasions. As the year passed, however, I began to adjust to life in Marietta, and school became more enjoyable. Making friends was much easier than I had expected. Soon I felt welcome, and within a relatively short time Marietta seemed like my home.

I lived in three or four different cities in Tennessee, and none can approach Cobb County, and Marietta in particular, in terms of atmosphere. My move taught me that change can be beneficial.

Cobb County's size, location, scenery, and atmosphere all contribute to making it a good place to live. But the area's most impressive quality is the richness of the opportunities it offers. I could never have attempted many of the things I've accomplished if I had remained in my hometown. I'm rarely at a loss for social activity, and if I am, it's because I'm not searching hard enough. I've definitely reaped the rewards of Cobb's abundant academic opportunities. Because my secondary school background was strong and thorough, I'm ready to receive the first-rate college education that preparation has made possible. Above all, however, is the opportunity my adopted home has given me to grow as a person. Cobb County's diversity allows a wide variety of experience, almost all of which contributes to healthy individual growth.

I'm sure my teen years were better because I lived in Marietta, and I'm equally sure I'll be better prepared to face the adult world, in Cobb County or wherever I live, because I grew up in a place that challenged and nurtured the best in me.

Trey Moores is a sophomore at Harvard University.

While these six incorporated communities provide the best threads for weaving the history of Cobb and while they play an integral role in the community's daily life and its atmosphere, most people, almost 80 percent, dwell in unincorporated Cobb. Until recent years, the fastest-growing part of the county was the area known as East Cobb, where thousands upon thousands of new citizens moved into subdivisions that sprang up like mushrooms, beautiful, various, entirely accommodating mushrooms in the colonial or French or contemporary or traditional styles.

East Cobb is rich in family life, with many subdivisions offering pools and tennis courts and community centers. In typical East Cobb neighborhoods, you find active neighborhood watch programs, swim and tennis teams, garden clubs, women's groups active in social and civic concerns, investment clubs—an array of activities that belies the myth of deadly isolation sometimes applied to suburban living. Despite the traditional view that living in an unincorporated, or non-urban, area means limited services and limited access to shopping, entertainment, and culture, East Cobb and other, similar sections of the county enjoy the full range of restaurants, shopping centers, and other "city" pleasures that their neighbors throughout Cobb and metropolitan Atlanta enjoy. East Cobb is also home to many business and professional opportunities, making it possible for residents to work close to home, certainly within the county, eliminating the long commute many associate with suburbia.

Of the unincorporated portions of Cobb, perhaps the two most clearly defined communities are Vinings and Mableton.

Vinings is as rich in history as any portion of Cobb. Located just across the Chattahoochee River from Atlanta's Buckhead neighborhood, in the southern part of Cobb, Vinings takes its name from an engineer who worked on the construction of the Western and Atlantic. The heart of "old Vinings" sits at the intersection of Paces Ferry and Paces Mill roads, both of which take their name from Hardy Pace, the first white settler across the Chattahoochee when the Cherokees were forced off the land.

The earliest inhabitants of what is now Vinings are believed to have been the Creeks, who are said to have named the Chattahoochee from their words *chatta*, meaning sparkling or flowered, and *ochee*, meaning rocks. The Creeks yielded the land to the Cherokees in the 1700s, and they remained until they were forced to leave under the treaty that stripped them of all their land in Georgia.

Sherman got his first glimpse of Atlanta's spires from Vinings Mountain, and during the battle for Atlanta messages by flag and torch were sent from there. Sherman and his troops entered the village on July 5, 1864, making the original Hardy Pace home their headquarters during their eleven-day stay. When they left to march on to Atlanta, they burned the house.

Pace, who is buried on Vinings Mountain, came to the area from North Carolina and began operating a ferry at the site of the present bridge across the Chattahoochee on U.S. 41. His flat-bottomed ferries were large enough for a horse and wagon; the river's current provided the power, and a bank-to-bank cable served as the guide for the ferry captain. Pace's business was so profitable that he was said to own all of Vinings, ten thousand acres bounded by Atlanta, Buckhead, and Smyrna.

In the late 1830s and the early 1840s, the Western and Atlantic track reached the settlement and a depot was built, a development that changed Vinings just as much as it transformed the other Cobb communities along the tracks. During Re-

construction, Governor Joseph Brown leased the W&A railroad and built five open-air pavilions, the most popular of which stood at the foot of Vinings Mountain. These pavilions became the site of society day-excursions by debutantes, eligible bachelors, and grande-dame chaperones. One prominent group that frequented the Vinings pavilion was the Every Tuesday Club. They bathed in crystal streams and danced in the pavilion.

On what is today called Stillhouse Road, Rufus Rose, a New York druggist, operated a still in Vinings. When Georgia went dry in 1908, his son, Randolph, moved the distillery to Chattanooga. Eventually, their business became the Seagram's Four Roses blend, per-

haps Vinings's most widely recognized export.

What was a fashionable retreat for city dwellers one hundred years ago is today a community of stately homes, splendid shopping, thriving business parks, outstanding restaurants, and first-class hotels. Men who can remember camping at the Boy Scouts' Camp Bert Adams may now work in the gleaming office towers that occupy some of the same land or live in the hundreds of luxury apartments also built there.

Mrs. Earle Carter Smith, a descendant of Hardy Pace, bought the Vinings pavilion in the forties, enclosed it, and converted it into antique shops, the beginning of modern-day Vinings's identity as a haven for shoppers and as an antique mecca. Smith and her sister Ruth Carter Vanneman are responsible for much of the community's historic preservation.

But there is also a question about what the future of Vinings should be. The "new" Vinings is stretching skyward, partly because land is scarce and costly, but residents are fiercely committed to maintaining the area's character despite the growth. Thus, the Homeowners' Association opposes the development of additional office buildings. Residents prefer developments such as the Vinings Jubilee, a gathering of more than twenty shops, totally in keeping with its historic locale in terms of decor and design.

While Vinings is perhaps Cobb's most coherently preserved representation of its past, Mableton may be a glimpse toward its future. Nonetheless, Mableton has its own historical roots that are both deep and quite evident in its current life.

The community is named for Scottish immigrant Robert Mable, who came to Georgia via Quebec and New York, having heard of the lottery for land, reportedly land that

housed gold. Originally heading toward Savannah, Mable eventually worked his way up the Chattahoochee, crossed the Green/Howell Ferry, operated on land that is now part of Six Flags over Georgia, and leased three hundred acres in southern Cobb County with visions of gold dancing in his head. The exact date of Mable's arrival is unknown, but by 1837 he had married Pheriby Aycock of Lithonia, and by 1843 he had built a sawmill and completed a plantation, called Plain House.

Later renamed the Mable House, his home was taken over by federal troops during the Civil War and used as a hospital. In 1881 a chief engineer for the Georgia Pacific Railway boarded there and named the railway station built nearby Mableton. Robert Mable's last surviving daughter, a Mableton schoolteacher until the early twentieth century, willed the home to a perpetual trust. The house has become

the hub of activity in development, improvement, and the arts for all of South Cobb.

The South Cobb Development Authority, the South Cobb Improvement Association, and the South Cobb Arts Alliance are all headquartered in the Mable House, marrying today's Cobb to yesterday's. The Mable family cemetery, located behind the house, serves as a constant reminder of the past in the midst of these organizations' dedicated efforts to preserve valuable history and to continue orderly progress and cultural development.

The South Cobb Development Authority defines South Cobb as bounded by the eastern limits of Austell and Powder Springs and the southern limits of Smyrna and the Fulton County line. The Improvement Association was formed in 1981, and the Development Authority soon followed. Now their strategies and actions for a "hub" area in Mableton are models for other areas of the county and state. As a large-scale cultural center, the Mable House creates a focal point for the community and has become the scene of perhaps the most intense community involvement in all of Cobb. The contributions of the area PTAs to the development of the Mable House and its projects already total more than fifty thousand dollars, just one sign of how pervasive the community's commitment to this planned growth and preservation movement is.

From 1912 to 1916 Mableton was, in fact, an incorporated city. The Bankhead Highway, its central artery, was paved in the 1930s. That same era saw phones and electricity reach area homes. In the forties, fifties, and sixties, small businesses began springing up to support the steadily growing population. In 1967 the opening of Six Flags over

Georgia provided a major economic boost.

Current plans call for widening Bankhead Highway to five lanes, opening the way for further development, refurbishing, and revitalization. Future growth plans focus on industry. South Cobb has more industrial acreage available than does the rest of the county. Thousands of acres of industrial parks are ready or almost ready for occupancy. These parks have been designed to be first-class, high-quality areas, with mostly brick buildings and extensive landscaping, in the manner of office parks.

The extension of the East-West Connector to South Cobb and perhaps across I-285 to Vinings will be a factor in the continued growth and

development of South Cobb. It will also link the two most clearly defined communities of South Cobb, completing a circle of past and future in today's careful strategy for keeping Cobb County the best of all possible worlds.

JACK BOONE

In the forties and early fifties, Cobb was rural. Life was simple. Nobody had a lot, but nearly everybody had enough. We were largely ordinary, hard-working folks—honest, trustworthy, devoted to family, mostly Christian, very dry. Social activities revolved around the churches. Progress didn't dominate our vocabulary. We were content.

Then it happened. We were in progress's path, a fact that did not escape ambitious young entrepreneurs with unshakeable faith—people like Bill Ward, who built Belmont Hills, then the largest shopping center in the South. Bill died a few years back, but he left a legacy of entrepreneurship to an entire generation of young builders, me included. He was a literal one-man Chamber of Commerce.

Another Cobb Countian of extraordinary vision was Commissioner Ernest Barrett. He properly forecast the progress that was to come and fought the old guard to get the county ready. He shocked our population by winning a $25 million bond referendum. We were afraid we'd never pay it off. But Ernest lived to see his visions fulfilled.

East Cobb was largely forest in those days. West Cobb was both forest and open land. There were probably more cows than people. The development of East Cobb into a community of higher-priced homes changed both the political profile and the lifestyle of the county. Talented people from the world over demanded and got the best in suburban living. In less than thirty years we were transformed—from a backward rural county to one of the Southeast's most sophisticated living areas.

Jack Boone is a retired realtor and building contractor who lives in Smyrna.

Maintaining The Vital Signs

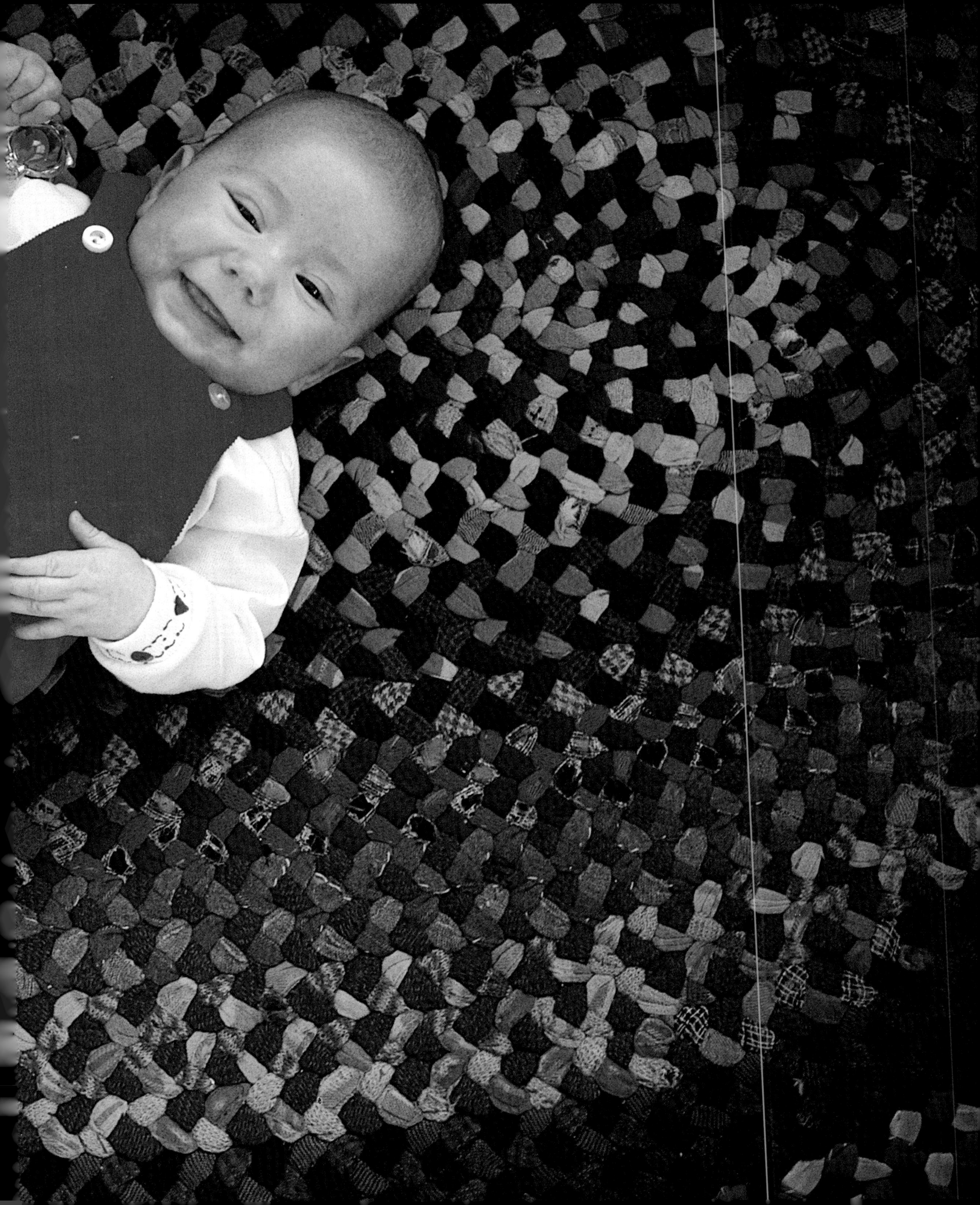

Thus, this is Cobb County: a great place to live and work—beautiful, rich in history, with a progressive, energetic atmosphere for business and economic development. How do we keep it that way?

As with any large, complex system of living, working, and growing, Cobb County requires a vast array of services and structures to maintain the vitality for which it is known and sought-after. The process of necessary maintenance begins with county and city government.

Cobb County is governed by a five-member board of commissioners, who serve staggered four-year terms. A county manager, employed by the commission, handles daily operations. Marietta, the seat of the county government, functions on the mayor-council model, as do the five other incorporated communities. Typically, mayors and city council members serve four-year terms, and daily operations fall to the city manager whom they appoint.

The county's general operating fund is derived primarily from taxes, license and permit fees, and service charges. Typical distribution of the overall fund falls along these guidelines: public safety, 30 percent; parks, libraries, and other community service, 17 percent; administrative services, 16 percent; judicial services, 14 percent; transportation, 11 percent; legislative and management services, 6 percent; community development, 4 percent; and agency grants, 2 percent. The commission's challenge is to improve and expand services while maintaining the county's tax rate, the second lowest in the metropolitan Atlanta area.

In order to improve the flow of information between government and citizens, the commission has established a Communications Office. One of its innovations is the videotaping of commission meetings for broadcast on cable television.

Since the eighties alone brought a 49 percent increase in the county's population, the commission has also established two new Government Service Centers to help meet burgeoning citizen needs in the eastern and southern areas of the county. The centers bring service closer to citizens. Designed as one-stop shops, the centers allow residents to pay water bills, purchase vehicle tags and transit-system tickets, purchase or renew business licenses, register to vote, and return library books, all in one central location. The centers also provide meeting rooms for community groups.

Through its agency grants program, the commission strives to extend its influence even more directly into the lives of citizens. Grants traditionally support arts programming and help to fund emergency aid organizations and hospitals. A new convention center, for the benefit of citizens and to draw convention business to the community, is in the planning stages. The Cobb Extension Service holds programs such as parenting classes, with the assistance of the commission's committee on children and youth.

A comprehensive Senior Service Center, the county's seventh, is under construction. These centers, funded by the county's senior services division, provide adult day care, transportation, and Meals on Wheels. In addition, the centers, in Acworth, Kennesaw, Marietta, and Smyrna, offer meeting rooms, dance floors, a ceramic kiln, and crafts and game rooms. An Aging Connection Hotline, another county service, can respond to immediate needs. Field trips, shopping excursions, and informational programs are also carried out under the auspices of senior services. A Senior Citizens Council represents eighty-seven clubs and organizations and serves as an umbrella agency to inform and serve older residents.

Cobb County was one of the state's first to develop a comprehensive land-use plan in compliance with the state's new growth strategies legislation. This plan will be the guide for land-use decisions well into the next century. A second Community Improvement District is planned for the Town Center/Barrett area in northwest Cobb. It will be

©Jane Gardner Preston

patterned after the successful model in the Cumberland/Galleria area, offering among other things a special taxing district that will generate revenues to address long-range development needs.

Cobb is entering the nineties with the first long-range solid waste management plan in the state. The plan includes reduction in waste by avoiding disposables and bulk packaging, reusing items whenever possible, and establishing a composting site for organic matter. All county documents will be printed on recycled paper, and an in-house recycling program has been instituted at commission headquarters. Multi-material drop-off sites are also part of the plan. The overall goal is to reduce total waste in Cobb by 40 percent within a decade.

The Cobb Clean Commission provides newspaper recycling bins at all county fire stations; in 1990 more than one million pounds of newspaper were recycled as a result. The commission also has a phosphorous control plan for protecting the water supply, including a ban on laundry detergents containing phosphates.

A similar mission created the Marietta Clean City Commission, charged with promoting environmental awareness through affiliation with the Keep America Beautiful and the Georgia Clean and Beautiful pro-

grams. As part of its effort to encourage all recycling, the commission, like its counterpart at the county level, provides recycling bins at city fire stations. The commission's mascot, the Marietta Muncher, is available to entertain and to inform children's groups about the consequences of littering and the benefits of recycling. Speakers for adult groups are also available. Along with volunteers, the Marietta Clean City Commission has planted trees in public areas, created a playground for handicapped children, con-

ducted numerous clean-ups of unsightly areas, and is working to restore the city's cemetery.

Cobb County government is also pioneering in the judicial arena with a program in advanced electronic confinement, designed to reduce inmate maintenance costs and to streamline the hearing process. Another judicial innovation is making education part of the legal process, through alcohol-awareness classes and sessions on truancy protocol.

Public safety is, of course, a primary concern of all citizens. Cobb was the first county in the metro area to take advantage of a funding mechanism that allows its 911 emergency unit to generate self-supporting revenues, thus freeing almost two million dollars from the general fund for additional public safety programs.

A Geographic Information System provides computerized mapping of every location in the county to allow quicker, more efficient emergency response. New fire stations and increased fire personnel have also meant an improved fire rating and a subsequent reduction in homeowners' insurance premiums.

More than thirty-five fire stations blanket the county. Austell, Marietta, and Smyrna have their own fire departments; the county department covers all other areas. Marietta has six stations; Smyrna, three; and

Austell, two. The first volunteer fire station opened in 1955. In 1971 the Board of Commissioners adopted a resolution that combined fire protection under a single chief. By 1977 the department had initiated a program to teach all fifth-graders in public and private schools the essentials of fire safety, a program since expanded to include first-graders as well.

The professionalism of fire protection services increased in 1979 when a recruit school opened to provide complete training for all new firefighters. The Cobb department became the first major fire department in the state to be certified by the Georgia Firefighter Standards and Training Council in 1980.

Through its own development and testing, the Cobb fire department created "Instant Firefighter," an inexpensive residential sprinkler system. Nineteen eighty-one saw the addition of a Hazardous Materials Team to the department's services, and in 1985 the Cobb Emergency Management Agency was placed under the fire department's direction to handle natural and man-made disasters.

In the mid-eighties the Emergency Medical Services Division was formed. All firefighters have since been trained to become state-certified EMTs; many are also licensed paramedics. A number of state-certified first-responder rescue units are also part of the Cobb County Fire Department. The 1986 installation of the computer-aided 911 dispatch system meant even greater efficiency in answering citizens' needs. In 1990 Cobb fire protection again led the way toward the future, becoming the first in the metro area to equip its rescue trucks with automatic heart defibrillators, a move that will increase the survival rate among victims of cardiac arrest.

The evolution from a simple

volunteer force in the mid-fifties to today's cutting-edge technology and services in the area of fire protection models the county's transformation from sleepy rural life to fast-paced contemporary growth and vitality. Cobb has learned well that growth in people and businesses without concomitant expansion of essential services and administrative procedures is unacceptable if a community is to maintain the quality of life that first attracted growth. The story of fire protection in the county is emblematic of the foresightful, responsible approach to growth that has made Cobb the highly desirable place it is.

More than three hundred employees staff the Cobb County Police Department, with another hundred or so working in the Sheriff's Department. In addition, all six incorporated towns have their own public safety departments. Cobb's crime rate is among the metro Atlanta area's lowest, and the solution rate for crimes committed within the county is higher than the national average.

The police department goes back to 1924, when it was established to handle traffic for the sheriff's department. The biggest problem in those days was trafficking in moonshine whiskey. The speed limit was thirty miles per hour, and there were few paved roads. By the early 1960s the county police department had transferred all its detective functions to the sheriff's department because of the large traffic volume on hundreds of miles of paved roads.

In 1969 detectives returned to the department. The Cobb Regional Police Academy, established in 1974, graduated more than five hundred officers from seventy-five agencies before closing in 1978. Nineteen seventy-four also brought the establishment of a Crime Prevention Unit and a reorganization into a

precinct structure. The Selective Traffic Program began in 1976, and in 1977 the SWAT unit was formed.

The eighties began with the formation of the Marietta-Cobb-Smyrna Drug Squad and the SCUBA Dive Rescue Team. The motorcycle unit debuted in 1984; 1985 brought the DUI Task Force and the 55-MPH Enforcement Program. The consolidation of Emergency Communications and the installation of the Enhanced-911 System in 1987 brought the police department into sync with the fire prevention program in being ready to make immediate, efficient response to the needs of county residents.

The police department's origins in Cobb's traffic needs in the 1920s is only one indication of the crucial role of transportation within the community. Any essentially suburban area is dependent on transportation in a unique way: the movement into and out of the area must be efficient for those whose work takes them away from the community itself; at the same time the transportation system should not disrupt the tranquil aspects of suburban life that are one of its biggest attractions.

The historical link between Cobb County's growth and development and transportation is clear in the stories of all its major communities—trains and ferries and tourism all suggest that transportation played a key role in the transformation of Cobb. The more recent developments of the interstate system and the emergence of Atlanta's Hartsfield International Airport as one of the world's busiest aviation centers have only intensified the connection between transportation and Cobb's growth.

The county boasts approxi-

mately seventeen hundred miles of roads, up more than 350 miles since 1980 alone. The maintenance of the seven thousand individual roads and 158 bridges that make up those miles is the responsibility of the Cobb County Department of Transportation. The department's plans for the future focus on widening two-lane roads to four lanes, replacing bridges, resurfacing streets, and improving intersections and sidewalks. An additional one-cent sales tax for roads was passed by county voters in 1985, leading to an investment of $440 million. In 1990 voters again supported the one-penny road tax in order to keep their roads in the best possible condition.

Until July 1989 Cobb County was the most populous area in the United States without a mass-transit system of any kind. The debut of the Cobb Community Transit system (CCT) remedied that situation. The first transit system in the U.S. to be fully accessible to handicapped passengers from its beginning, the CCT's remarkable success has astounded industry analysts and become a model studied by other communities across the land. Two years before projections, the CCT carried its millionth passenger, less than one year after operations began. Average weekday ridership is almost

eight thousand, and the service is as good as it is used: less than two complaints for every ten thousand passengers.

Through CCT's regular and express routes, Cobb County riders can connect with Atlanta's MARTA system and travel much of the metropolitan area without using their own vehicles. The fleet of thirty-six buses features fabric-upholstered seats, public address systems, and wheelchair lifts in all vehicles. The express buses have reading lights and parcel racks as well.

Even before the bus system began operation, CCT sponsored a rideshare program to match citizens for carpooling. In operation since 1986, the rideshare program has matched some four thousand commuters.

But CCT is not content to rest on its success. Instead, officials are looking toward the future, experimenting with ways to make their system work harder and better for the county. In May 1990 CCT added a vanpool program to its services. Nine vans are made available to commuters with common work destinations and home origins. CCT can generate match lists for vanpool users in an effort to accommodate people commuting from areas without sufficient ridership for regular bus service. Plans call for fifty vans to be in operation by the end of 1992.

CCT's demand/response system will debut early in 1992, offering priority service to the elderly and handicapped and to the general public in rural areas. The concept is similar to taxi service and is aimed at the increasing number of senior citizens who choose to "age in place" rather than move to a retirement community. Riders in the program make reservations. Then CCT pairs them with others in their area with similar needs and schedules and sends a small bus to meet the group's

transportation needs.

In cooperation with the Cobb Community Improvement District, CCT has established programs to coordinate employer-based transportation options, such as flex time, vanpools, carpools, transit fare subsidies, and shuttles.

Although Cobb's easy access to Hartsfield Airport is one of the county's strong selling points to businesses considering opening or relocating here, Hartsfield is not the only air facility making Cobb easily accessible. McCollum Field at the Cobb County Airport is a general aviation facility serving the more than three hundred aircraft based there and upwards of 144,000 take-offs and landings each year. Plans for McCollum do not include expanding into commercial service; rather, it will remain a reliever airport, to handle the overflow of smaller traffic from nearby Hartsfield.

Thirty acres have recently been developed at the airport for parking and hangar space. The single runway extends fifty-six hundred feet, is lighted for night traffic, and can accommodate planes up to thirty-five thousand pounds, which includes propeller or jet twin-engine, seven-passenger planes. Recent improvements, funded primarily by the Federal Aviation Administration and secondarily by the county, will increase the plane space at McCollum by 30 percent, to more than four hundred planes.

Owned by the county, the airport is run by two fixed-base operators, who provide everything for airplanes and their owners that a marina does for boats and boat owners.

McCollum, the fourth-busiest airport in Georgia, is a non-controlled field, meaning it has no FAA control tower. The number of aircraft based at McCollum is the third highest in the state, and a 1989 analysis concluded that the airport's total annual economic impact on the area exceeds thirty-five million dollars.

Located in Kennesaw, McCollum Field is a particular advantage to development in the fast-growing northwestern quadrant of the county and in the Town Center/Barrett business-retail-entertainment-residential district.

One place Cobb residents are going is to the library. In the eighties the library system doubled its capacity while use tripled. In 1989 circulation figures reached 1,564,873; the growth rate in circulation had reached approximately 100,000 volumes per year.

The origins of the county's library system are in the Civil War years, specifically in an organization called the Young Men's Debating and Library Association. By 1874 the group had changed its name to the Young Men's Literary Association, and in 1882 the Franklin Lending Library opened. Men, however, did not have the only impact on the genesis of libraries in Cobb County. Sarah Freeman Clarke began a library in her home on Whitlock Avenue in Marietta. Her operating funds came from subscriptions and from contributions by nineteenth-century authors such as Oliver Wendell Holmes. By 1893 the Sarah Freeman Clarke library had been installed in a permanent home on Church Street, just off the Marietta Square.

In 1957 various small libraries merged to form the Cobb County/Marietta Public Library. JoAnne Sutton, a former library director, was instrumental in the system's growth, and a branch in Powder Springs now bears her name. In 1957 Kennesaw

residents helped the county purchase its first bookmobile so that they didn't have to rely solely on the state bookmobile. The library system came under the county's budget and administrative umbrella in 1969.

Almost 450,000 books and media holdings now call the Cobb/Marietta Library System home, scattered among fifteen branch libraries and the new central library opened in 1989. This eight-million-dollar, sixty-four-thousand-square-foot facility brings Cobb County to the forefront of the state's biggest and best library systems. Among the services offered at the libraries are story hours and other children's programs, summer reading clubs, an interlibrary loan system, book discussion groups, films, puppet shows, a phone-a-story line, a reserve system, and computerized services. Voter and selective service registration may be done at any branch; tax forms, both state and federal, are also available, as are free publications, such as *Creative Loafing*, a weekly tabloid that features current cultural and recreation opportunities throughout the metro area.

More than eleven hundred periodicals are available on computer or microfiche, and the library makes available the *Wall Street Journal* and other publications of concern to the business community. Meeting rooms are also provided to nonprofit organizations at no charge. The Georgia Room is a special collection of local history and local interest publications.

The city of Smyrna operates its own library. Established in 1936, the Smyrna library is Georgia's oldest city-operated library. Its current annual budget of approximately $250,000 is funded entirely by the city. The current five-thousand-square-foot library building, designed in 1961 for fourteen thousand

volumes, is now jammed with fifty-three thousand. The new library being constructed as part of Smyrna's extensive downtown revitalization will comfortably house 106,000 volumes in its twenty-seven-thousand square feet.

On December 1, 1975, more than forty concerned citizens of Cobb County completed a training program and began operation of the Cobb County Rape Crisis Center, which became part of the crisis intervention program at the YWCA of Cobb County in 1982. In 1978 the Cobb YWCA had opened the state's

first shelter for battered women in Marietta, and the addition of the rape crisis program broadened the spectrum of services available to women who have been victims of physical assault and domestic violence. Among the services offered by these programs are individual and group counseling, legal advocacy, twenty-four-hour-a-day crisis hotlines, and other peer and professional support. In 1989 the YWCA's shelter for battered women and their children moved into new headquarters, built through a massive community fund-raising campaign. The new shelter has ten bedrooms, laundry facilities, a kitchen, and a play area. In 1991 the YWCA began a child-care service for the clients of its crisis intervention program.

Another Cobb County social agency has achieved national recognition for its work with the homeless and other citizens struggling to cope with the essentials of life. Ministries United in Service and Training (MUST) began as an overnight shelter for the homeless, housed in a building off the Marietta Square that allowed the organization to serve fewer than two dozen people each night. Today, MUST operates the Elizabeth Inn, a facility that can serve more than three times as many men, women, and children as the original site could. In addition to the shelter, MUST offers a noon-time kitchen for needy citizens, a day shelter for women and children, health screenings, job referrals, and many other key services to its clients.

During the winter months the Marietta/Cobb Winter Shelter Board oversees an additional shelter for the homeless housed at Christ Episcopal Church in Kennesaw. Christ Episcopal's parishioners took on the sponsorship of the shelter in 1989, when its original site was bulldozed to prepare for a construction project, and have maintained a strong commitment to this particular mission within their community. Cobb County Emergency Aid, the Salva-

tion Army, and the Good Samaritan Shelter, which houses families while they get on their feet financially and can live independently within the community, are other examples of the bigness of Cobb's heart and its commitment to serving the needs of every citizen.

Almost every civic organization and club known to man and woman has a branch or branches in Cobb County: Lions, Kiwanis, Rotary, Junior League, American Association of University Women—you name it, Cobb has it. These organizations involve the business and social communities in the larger social needs of the area to produce an enormous amount of significant work for the betterment of Cobb and the enrichment of all lives.

One organization of more specialized interest is the Cobb Landmarks and Historical Society. Founded in 1975, the society currently has five hundred members. One of its goals is to educate the community about its historical resources, partly through functioning as a networking agency for all the county's historical groups. The society has a slide presentation and a speakers bureau available for presentations to schools and organizations throughout Cobb. Involved in the annual Christmas Marietta Pilgrimage Home Tour and the Past and Repast Luncheon lecture series at the Marietta Welcome Center, the society is currently focusing its energies on the renovation of the historic Root House.

The house, built in 1839 as a residence for William Root, Marietta's first pharmacist, is one of Cobb's oldest structures still standing. Originally constructed on Church Street, the house was moved to Lemon Street when the Clarke Library was built. The restoration began with another move, to the intersection of Polk Street and the

Marietta Parkway. Plans call for the Root House to be a museum of the 1840s, complete with a period garden, when the renovation is complete.

Another civic organization that

has been an effective leader in the "adaptive use" movement that marries progress and preservation is the Marietta Educational Garden Center. Housed in an antebellum home on Kennesaw Avenue, the center encourages respect for the past and its treasures at the same time it looks forward with its recycling and other programs designed to create the best possible future for Cobb County. The adaptation of older homes for contemporary purposes is also evidenced in the restored homes along Washington, Church, and Lawrence streets in Marietta, many of which house law offices and other businesses.

ealthcare is another essential element of a community's infrastructure. If someone is going to be sick, Cobb County is a good place to do so. Facilities include seven public health centers, four hospitals with a total of more than one thousand beds, and nine nursing homes with almost one thousand total beds. Special facilities for treatment of mental health problems and substance abuse provide almost three hundred additional beds. More than three hundred physicians and two hundred dentists practice in Cobb County.

The oldest and largest of the hospitals is Kennestone, part of the state's second-largest hospital organization, which serves more than 100,000 patients per year. The county's other full-service facility is the Cobb Hospital and Medical Center, which opened its doors in 1968. Like most forward-thinking healthcare facilities, Cobb's leaders are developing a number of programs in the area of preventive medicine: walking programs, fitness centers, screening programs that they carry into the community. The role of the hospital within the community continues to change and grow. No longer designed only to treat the critically ill, these hospitals want to make healthcare and their role in it integral to the daily lives of Cobb's citizens.

Every medical need from neonatal critical care to chemical abuse to eating disorders to sophisticated cardiac procedures to gerontology can be met in Cobb County by world-class professionals using the latest high-technology equipment available. Ridgeview Institute is world-renowned for its treatment of physicians and others suffering from chemical dependency, and Brawner Psychiatric Institute offers valuable mental health and other services to adults and adolescents, who can attend an accredited school on the Brawner grounds while they receive treatment.

erhaps the most important element of a community's infrastructure is its school system. Almost nowhere in the United States can students, from kindergarten through college, find greater educational opportunities than in Cobb County. The community's involvement in education is a matter of national record: Cobb native Alice McLellan Birney organized the nation's first PTA in 1897. The first branch in her home county was established in Marietta in 1919.

The county's elementary and secondary schools are governed by two systems: the Cobb County Schools and the Marietta City Schools. Both are accredited by the Southern Association of Colleges and Schools. With seventy-seven schools and more than sixty-six thousand students, the Cobb system is the state's second largest and one of the largest in the entire country. Nine schools and approximately five thousand students make up the Marietta system. All public elementary and middle schools have individual parent conferences as part of the academic schedule, and high-school students' parents meet with an advisor when their child enters ninth grade to plan his or her curriculum for the high-school years. All Cobb County and Marietta City schools offer after-school programs for children of working parents.

The Cobb County Schools include fifty-two elementary schools, fifteen middle schools (and one alternative middle school), and twelve high schools (and an alternative high school). The system employs seventy-seven hundred people, including almost four thousand teachers, approximately 45 percent of whom hold a master's degree or higher. An innovative effort, the Mentor Teacher Program, pairs beginning teachers one-on-one with experienced master

teachers in an effort to attract and retain the highest quality faculty and to recognize dedicated superior teachers.

The Cobb County Schools are ranked second in the state in terms of academic achievement and thirty-sixth in the nation. A sampling of indicators reinforces these statistics of excellence. In one recent year Cobb's schools produced: fifty-nine National Merit Scholars, two National Fitness Demonstration Center schools, a National Wildlife Federation Campus, seven members of the All-Star High-School Jazz Band, and dozens of athletic, artistic, scholastic, and teaching awards. Within the system, thirteen schools have received the Georgia Schools of Excellence recognition, and seven schools have been recognized as National Schools of Excellence.

Instruction emphasizes composition and critical thinking in all disciplines. High expectations for student performance in strong academic programs means regular homework assignments; the result is consistent performance above the national average on standardized tests and above achievement levels predicted by students' ability levels.

North Cobb High participates in an innovative Satellite Educational Resources Consortium project that allows students to study Japanese through satellite transmission and to participate in interactive science seminars. The Cobb County Center for Excellence in the Performing Arts is open, through audition, to all Cobb high-school students with outstanding talent in vocal music, dance, and drama.

The elementary schools range in size from the smallest, Fitzhugh Lee in Smyrna, with 238 students to the largest, Mt. Bethel in Marietta, with 1,444. Middle schools range from Mableton's Lindley, enrollment 693, to Powder Springs's Tapp, en-

rollment 1,379. The smallest high school, Pebblebrook, with 923 students, is also in Mableton. The largest high school is also probably the most unusual of the county's schools: McEachern, enrollment 2,047, is the only privately endowed public school in the state. McEachern, also the county's oldest school, has a closed-circuit television station on its sixty-two acre campus.

Adult education is also part of the Cobb system. That program offers free English as a Second Language (ESOL) classes for those sixteen and older not enrolled in a high school; Graduate Equivalency Diploma (GED) classes and tests; classes leading to an adult-education high-school diploma; and a variety of computer and business-oriented classes.

Another feature of the Cobb system is its nationally recognized Community School Program, which offers county residents after-school enrichment, recreational, and vocational classes, and a wide variety of activities designed to make the schools a vibrant part of community life at many levels. The Marietta City Schools, in a joint venture with the Marietta Parks and Recreation Department, also offer evening and Saturday classes to the community at a small charge.

Within the traditional education framework, Marietta has seven elementary schools, one middle school, and one high school. Three of the nine have been named Georgia Schools of Excellence. Nineteen ninety-two will mark the one hundredth anniversary of the Marietta schools. In a kind of early celebration, all system schools were equipped with computer labs for the 1990-91 academic year. One reason for the success of the city's school system is the contribution of Marietta Power to the revenues for operating the schools. Because the city has its own power company to generate part of the school budget, taxes within the city can remain the lowest in metro Atlanta without education's suffering in the least.

On achievement tests, Marietta students generally perform approximately one year above the national level for all grades and subjects. The system's teacher-to-student ratio is 1:24, and the per-pupil expenditure is among the state's highest. The starting salary for teachers is the fourth-highest in the state, and across the board teacher salaries are approximately 20 percent higher than the state system's base salary guidelines. Approximately 67 percent of Marietta's teachers hold master's degrees or higher.

The PTA is four thousand strong, one indication of the community's active involvement in its schools. Another is the system's 100 percent participation in the Partners in Education program that teams schools with area businesses. Perhaps the best indication of the strong reputation of the city's schools is that each year finds about one hundred "tuition" students enrolled. Because they live outside the city limits of Marietta and are ineligible to attend otherwise, they pay for the privilege of being educated by the city's schools.

In addition to its two public school systems, Cobb offers some excellent private education opportunities as well. Among the most interesting is the Georgia Japanese Language School. Staffed by fifty teachers employed by a nonprofit organization, Saturday classes from nine A.M. until four P.M. instruct children from the ages of six to fifteen in Japanese. More than three hundred of the school's almost six hundred students attend classes at Lindley Middle School in Mableton. Primarily aimed at the children of the metro area's Japanese population, the school is open to anyone who wants to study a range of subjects in Japanese. The German Saturday School, a similar program, operates at the Dickerson Middle School.

Cobb's oldest private school is the Walker School. The fully accredited institution caps its enrollment at 750 students in order to maintain a close family environment. Founded in 1957 as St. James Day School by the Reverend Joseph T. Walker, rector of St. James Episcopal Church in Marietta, the school changed its name in 1971 and moved to its current building, in Marietta, in 1977. The school no longer has any religious affiliation.

Eighty percent of its student body comes from Cobb County. Students from pre-kindergarten through grade twelve study under fifty faculty members on a fifteen-acre campus. Admissions testing is required, and transfer students also need to provide transcripts and a teacher or principal recommendation.

Foreign languages are taught in all grades. The school is known for excellence in the visual and performing arts and is home to a semi-professional theater group. The average SAT score of Walker students is eleven hundred. The teacher-to-student ratio is 1:17, and 100 percent

of graduates are accepted at the college of their choice.

The fully accredited Mt. Paran Christian School, also in Marietta, was founded in the late 1970s at Mt. Paran Church of God in Atlanta. The school moved to Marietta in 1986, where its sixty-five-acre site houses

two three-story classroom wings, a full-service kitchen, a gymnasium, a thirty-five-hundred-seat auditorium, a full-scale media center and library, tennis courts, and soccer, baseball, and softball fields.

Classes for three-year-olds through grade twelve enroll roughly

650 students. The typical graduating class numbers forty. Although the school is affiliated with the Church of God, its doctrine is not taught in the classroom and students needn't practice that faith. The school fields teams for interscholastic competition in men's baseball, basketball, soccer, and tennis and in women's softball, basketball, and tennis.

Even when students finish their twelve years of compulsory education, they need not leave Cobb County to continue learning. The county is home to five institutions of higher learning.

The largest of these is Kennesaw State College, the largest senior college in the University System of Georgia. Kennesaw State offers both bachelor's and master's degrees in a number of fields, including business and education, as well as the traditional arts and sciences. Cobb's other senior college is the Southern College of Technology, which offers associate's, bachelor's, and master's degrees in a variety of technical fields. In addition to these schools, Chattahoochee Technical Institute and the North Metro Technical Institute, both two-year schools offering vocational training and college-transfer courses, and Life Chiropractic College, the largest such institution in the world, call Cobb County home.

Kennesaw State and Southern Tech have become the "adopted" alma maters of many Cobb citizens who graduated from other institutions. For example, Fred Bentley has donated volumes from his rare book collection to both institutions. At Kennesaw State the rare book room

bears his name in tribute to his contribution.

Kennesaw State began as Kennesaw Junior College in 1966, with an enrollment of one thousand students. Ten thousand students now attend the four-year senior college, which enters the nineties with a new ten-million-dollar building to house its School of Business Administraton, the state's third largest. The new building will also house the department of computer sciences and the Small Business Development Center.

Kennesaw State College's site was chosen because of the projected route of I-75's northward expansion during the young turks' period of development and forward thinking in the mid-sixties. Horace W. Sturgis, who became the college's first president, was among the most vocal and persuasive advocates for its creation. The county promised the Board of Regents, which governs the University System of Georgia, land, roads, and utilities for the college. The county also paid for the construction of the original campus buildings, thus presenting the regents with a completed campus at no cost. The location has, of course, proved prescient: Kennesaw's campus is right in the middle of the Town Center/Barrett development area.

Senior college status was granted in the seventies, and Betty L. Siegel, the college's president, is the first and only woman to hold that office within the University System.

In 1989 *U.S. News & World Report* listed Kennesaw State as an "up-and-coming" school, one of only thirty-two nationwide so designated. The school aims to be a prototype of the college of the future, where professional adults return for advanced training and degrees that will help

them compete in a service- and information-oriented society. Fifty-one percent of KSC's undergraduates are older than twenty-three; many are in their thirties and forties, taking night and weekend classes.

Recent programs initiated at KSC include the Burruss Institute of Public Service, founded in 1988 to help local governments improve their services; the Family Business Forum, a small-business development program now imitated nationwide; and a very active International Affairs program, that includes a major in international studies, connections with a broad array of international businesses, and trips to a variety of international destinations for students and faculty and local citizens. Kennesaw's visual arts department, added to its offerings in 1986, is typical of the growth pattern of the school's programs. From its inception, in less than five years, the program has grown to accommodate more than 150 majors. Although some institutions have cut programs in visual and performing arts during the same era, Kennesaw State is successfully expanding in these areas, partly because of its location in Cobb County, a community the college sees as dedicated to the arts.

Begun as a junior college in 1948, Southern Technical Institute was first housed at the U.S. Naval Air Station in Chamblee and operated as a branch of Georgia Tech, emphasizing applied technology. When Cobb's leaders promised land, roads, and utilities, the same strategy that would later get them Kennesaw College, the Board of Regents agreed to move the facility. The Marietta campus opened in 1961; in the 1970s the school was elevated to senior-college status and made independent of Georgia Tech.

Four thousand students call Southern Tech's two-hundred-acre campus home during their college

years. The school's philosophy that students learn by doing is reflected in the emphasis on laboratory work—the school has sixty modern labs—and in the selection of faculty with strong academic credentials *and* industry experience. The courses in the Southern Tech curriculum are structured to create a "real world" atmosphere, and all qualified engineering technology students may participate in the co-op program that puts them to work as they continue to learn. Southern Tech's 15 percent African-American enrollment is the second-highest of any engineering technology school in the country.

With two- and four-year degrees in ten areas and two graduate programs, Southern Tech has created exciting changes in the scope of technical education in the South. Social and professional organizations, cultural programs, and a strong arts-and-sciences curriculum reinforce and supplement the technical studies for which the school is noted.

The school's mission is to meet the needs of Georgia's citizens and industries for engineering technology and related instruction at the college level. But Southern Tech also recognizes and honors its responsibility to serve the "whole student" through strong programs in the humanities, social and natural sciences, mathematics, and communications and through an environment that fosters inquisitiveness, problem-solving, and a desire for continued learning. In addition to their classroom experience, Southern

Southern College of Technology

Kennesaw State College

Tech students can enrich their learning experience through participation in twelve fraternities and sororities, thirty-four other student organizations, and an on-campus newspaper and radio station.

During the 1980s Southern Tech produced more graduates with bachelor's degrees in engineering technology than any other college in the nation. But, because only 5 percent of Georgia's high-school gradu-

to provide technical and multilingual assistance to Georgia's export industry and to foreign companies located in the state. The center is dedicated to increasing international trade to and from Georgia and is known for its innovative business services and its ability to solve complex problems in the areas of overseas marketing, sales, and service.

Groundbreaking for a new student center at Southern Tech is

ment rate for graduates.

Among its more innovative ideas is the Employee Training Program, which provides employees with a foundation for assuming additional responsibilities at an accelerated rate. This goal can be reached through on-site training, on-campus training, custom-designed programs, or a combination of these options. Other programs include an LPN/RN bridge program in cooperation with

ates choose to study engineering and engineering technology fields at the college level, the school has begun a program for the state's elementary students and teachers, the Georgia Youth Science and Technology Center. Plans call for thirty regional labs to bring the wonders of science and technology to young students and their teachers to promote interest in these disciplines.

Other innovative programs include the W. Clair Harris Apparel and Textile Center of Excellence, a teaching laboratory for students planning to enter the apparel and textile industries. A perfect example of business, government, and education cooperation, the Harris Center serves business and industry as well as students through demonstrations. Also housed at Southern Tech is the World Technology Center, designed

scheduled for the near future. The $6.5 million project will enhance the quality of life on the campus and further the school's ability to meet its mission.

Chattahoochee Technical Institute, formerly called Marietta Cobb Tech, was established in 1961 and moved to its current campus in 1963. On July 1, 1987, its new name was officially adopted. The two-year technical school provides training in twenty fields of applied technology, awarding degrees in four areas, diploma programs, and continuing education courses. Its two newest associate's degrees are in computer programming and law enforcement. During its history Chattahoochee Tech has provided successful career preparation to more than 100,000 men and women and can boast of a 97 percent place-

Kennesaw State College and a full-time cooperative program for high-school seniors, placing them in the workplace as they continue their high-school curriculum.

North Metro Technical Institute opened its doors in 1989, with the mission of enhancing the area's skilled labor pool. It served more than one thousand students in its first year. Located on a fifty-acre campus in Acworth, in the heart of the county's projected high-growth area, North Metro Tech was conceived and designed as a "Showcase of Technology." Four brand-new high-tech buildings with 140,000 square feet and state-of-the-art equipment provide the ideal setting for learning. The faculty bring industry experience as well as advanced degrees to their jobs.

Diploma and associate degree

programs are offered, along with continuing education classes, GED classes and testing, and industry-specific training, including on-site training requested by businesses and industries. Through a cooperative program with Floyd College in Rome, technical courses successfully completed at North Metro Tech can be counted toward an Associate of Applied Science degree from Floyd, thus combining the advantages of hands-on technical education and a broad-based traditional college program.

North Metro Tech offers job placement assistance to its graduates and a unique warranty of its graduates to their employers. Both North Metro and Chattahoochee Tech participate in Georgia's Quick Start program, providing new or expanding companies with employee training at no cost.

Life College of Chiropractic, founded in 1975 by Sid E. Williams, who serves as its president, taught twenty-two students from a storefront when it opened its doors. Now almost two thousand students from thirty-five nations attend classes on its sixty-acre campus in Marietta. Williams's goal is to spread chiropractic medicine—and its theory that the body will heal itself if the bones in the spine are "adjusted" to remove encumbrances to proper nervous function—around the globe.

Williams believes that a climate of enthusiasm kindles the desire for excellence in any pursuit. The vibrant campus life at the college includes more than fifty fraternal, service, and social organizations, as well as a robust athletic program of thirteen extramural teams in addition to the school's championship rugby team, famous not only for its skill but for its practice of providing on-field adjustments for teammates and opponents.

In fall 1990 Life College's graduate school of sports science opened, the first step toward the school's becoming Life University of Chiropractic. The almost evangelical fervor of Williams's belief in his school and his science has led to the opening of Life Chiropractic College West in San Francisco in 1981 and to South Korea's acceptance of the Life Around the World initiative in 1986. Life College staffs a clinic, by invitation, at Taegu University in Korea. Research programs are also underway at universities in India and Rwanda. Two Life doctors are at work in Burkina Faso, and three are on the staff of the China Academy of Traditional Chinese Medicine in Beijing, at the request of the Chinese government. Negotiations are ongoing for initiatives in Brazil, the U.S.S.R., Mauritius, and Egypt.

In many ways the world comes to Cobb to be educated, as evidenced by the Japanese and German Saturday schools and the significant international student enrollments at Kennesaw State, Southern Tech, and Life College; Cobb County is also reaching out to the world, through international programs in the colleges and even in the high schools, making today's education a model for tomorrow's world.

The pulse of a healthy community can be checked at a number of points: government services, social agencies, civic organizations, schools. Touch any of these points in Cobb lightly or dig deep beneath the surface. Either way, you'll find a vibrant, growing, well-cared-for community ready to serve its citizens in the broadest and most specific ways. An old Temptations' song says, "We're doing fine on Cloud Nine." In Cobb County folks can stay much closer to home and get that same feeling. We're doing fine right here. And we're ready to carry that feeling into the next century. We'll be doing fine in 2001, 2010, and beyond.

TOM KEENE

When I first visited Kennesaw State College for a job interview in 1973, Interstate 75 wasn't even started in North Cobb. The college was surrounded by woods and pastures. Having grown up on a dairy farm, I loved it. Our first house was a rental deep in the woods. No neighbors in sight. You could take a shower in the summer and walk outside to dry off. It was most agreeable.

Nearly twenty years later, I still find both the mild climate and the woodsy quality of Cobb's landscape quite appealing. I like the fact that there are enough people within a generation or two of agricultural life to give the area a slower pace and a calmer approach to most things.

I have also enjoyed Cobb's growth and change even though it can be unsettling at times. Growth constantly opens up new possibilities for us at the college, making it an exciting place to work. The area has become much more multi-ethnic, multi-racial, and international. As a person with a professional interest in different cultures, I really enjoy these changes. The people of Cobb continue to be generous and accepting to newcomers, so I expect to see more and more cultural diversity in the years ahead. I'm looking forward to it.

Tom Keene is Director of International Programs and Professor of History at Kennesaw State College.

In the 1990-91 academic year, every Cobb County public elementary school was paired with a community business in the Partners in Education program, the brainchild of The Cobb Chamber of Commerce. The concept serves two important functions: first, the business supports the school in any number of ways that vary greatly from school to school and business to business: second, the business and its employees serve as mentors to students, are concerned models of adult success and commitment to work and community.

This program, which touches the lives of almost every school child in the county, is but one example of the business community's involvement in the larger community that it serves. Businesses that are Partners in Education agree to recognize and motivate students, recognize teachers, promote community service, and foster appreciation of business.

A good example of how the program works is the relationship between Murdock Elementary School and the Pacesetter Steel Service Company. Where education is concerned, Pacesetter lives up to its name. In 1990 it sponsored the third annual career day for fourth- and fifth-graders at Murdock. Pacesetter employees oversee participating students while they sell steel, place ads, practice hiring, and attend department-head meetings. The object is to teach students how corporations operate and what is required of workers.

©Jane Gardner Preston

Students must apply for the position they want within the Pacesetter organization. In 1990 fourth-grader J. P. Fournier snared the presidency by stapling his report card to his application and getting a recommendation from his third-grade teacher. Abby Russo, a fifth-grader, won the director of marketing position by citing training in dinner discussions with her dad, Steven Russo, president of his own marketing firm. Abby came to Pacesetter with slick business cards for the "Murdock Consulting Group, A Division of Pacesetter Steel." Scott Griggs, another fifth-grader, won a shot at sales with statistics and spunk. He also leaned on his experience with computers, calculators, and telephones.

The career day idea has proved so successful that other businesses, such as Kroger and Community Bank & Trust, have begun to imitate it. But Pacesetter's commitment to

Murdock goes beyond this single exciting day. Every Pacesetter employee spends a minimum of four hours in service at the school each academic year. They tutor, read to kids, conduct travelogs, lead ceremonies. Pacesetter is also active in an anti-drug campaign that has become the model for the national "Operation Know" program.

Calvin Coolidge's famous statement that "The business of America is business" certainly applies to Cobb County—Cobb is a business mecca. But one could paraphrase Coolidge's epigram and say something equally true about businesses in Cobb County: "The business of Cobb County business is Cobb County." The Partners in Education program is but one specific example of how businesses here strive to give back to the community that sustains them.

While the growth of the county has been phenomenal by any mea-

sure, the growth of business and business opportunities has been particularly remarkable. In the eighties alone, job opportunities increased at twice the rate of population growth. Almost 100,000 jobs were added to Cobb's economy in the last decade alone, and the county's unemployment rate is consistently among the lowest in the metro area. Seventeen thousand business licenses were issued in 1989, up 682 from the previous year. By 2010 employment opportunities are expected to increase by 320 percent, resulting in an estimated 406,000 jobs. The number of workers commuting to jobs *within* Cobb County will have risen by 165 percent. The work force will number more than 140,000. Forty-five percent of them will work within the county.

A number of factors clearly contribute to the rapid, continuing growth of businesses in Cobb. Its proximity to Atlanta, combined with the high percentage of undeveloped land in its 346-square-mile area, are perhaps the most obvious. Also important are the abundant natural resources, including the Chattahoochee River and Lake Allatoona. The traditional concept of suburban safety, borne out by law enforcement statistics, is another factor, as perhaps is the relative homogenity of the population. Pleasant living conditions paired with easy access to almost anywhere in the world—thanks to nearby Hartsfield —make for a strong inducement, as does the commitment to *quality* development, as opposed to development for its own sake. Finally, Cobb offers its businesses one of the strongest possible advocates and supporters in its cohesive, active Chamber of Commerce.

The philosophy behind the development of the Barrett complex in the northern part of the county is typical of Cobb and of why businesses flock here. At Barrett a founding premise was to keep "the fast-buck people out." The people they wanted in were those committed to high-quality participation in the area's vision of the future.

One of Cobb's earliest success

stories in the business arena belongs to the Brumby Chair Company. Established in 1875, the company manufactured a rocking chair that quickly became world-famous and still graces the living rooms and front porches of people far and wide.

A trip to the Marietta Square provides a glimpse of a business firmly connected to Cobb's past and its present. DuPre's has been operating at the same location just off the square since 1867. Founded by the Anderson family, the store was sold to H. N. DuPre in 1927. The current owner is his grandson. Over the years the store has sold hardware, general merchandise, feed and seed, farm implements, groceries, boats, appliances, and lighting fixtures. At one time it functioned as a cotton broker, selling directly to English manufacturers. In recent years the focus of DuPre's has been appliances and lighting; in 1990 H. N.'s grandson sold the appliance side of the business, but he's still there, selling lighting fixtures where his grandfather worked.

The link between history and business evidences itself in other ways, as well. Although Cobb is clearly no longer a farm community, one of its large business enterprises clearly reflects its agricultural roots. Tip Top Poultry, begun in 1953 by Chester A. Austin and the late A. L. Burruss, processes thirty-five hundred heavy breeder hens and roosters per day. Its annual sales exceed thirty million dollars. The company employs four hundred in Marietta, as well as another two hundred in Polk County, and owns a fleet of sixty vehicles. Not exactly a small farmer scratching subsistence from the soil, but Tip Top is a modern descendant of those early settlers. In fact, in the company's infancy, Austin and Burruss would catch the birds, process them, load them onto their single truck, and go sell them—all themselves, as if they were, in fact, independent farmers drawing sustenance from the land.

Joining the "homegrown" businesses such as DuPre's and Tip Top are the "transplants," those companies that began elsewhere but decided to move, bag and baggage, to Cobb. Typical of such firms is the Electrolux Corporation, which moved its corporate headquarters to Cobb in 1988. Cobb provided better, easier access to travel than Electrolux's original home, Stamford, Connecticut, especially since their main pension plants are located in the Southeast. Also influential in the decision to relocate were the potential for increased operating efficiency, the lower cost of living in Cobb, and the higher quality of life.

Sometimes new enterprises echo ancient themes in Cobb's story. A good example is Six Flags over Georgia. The amusement park opened on June 7, 1967, after an investment of $13,656,151 in construction and development. The rewards were almost immediate: in the first season of operation 1.2 million people visited the park. Operating for 187 days in 1989, the park hosted 2,350,000. Six Flags receives more than seven thousand applications for seasonal employment each year and is the largest single-location employer of teens in Georgia.

And, of course, it hearkens back to the old days when tourism made Cobb an economic force to be reckoned with before the Civil War and again afterwards.

Old standbys of the Cobb business scene do not stand still. Lockheed Aeronautical Systems is moving its corporate headquarters from Burbank, California, to Marietta, and the company is also consolidating plane-building operations from its Palmdale, California, plant in Marietta. The end result will be 3,150 new Marietta jobs by 1992.

Business and government are not completely separate entities in Cobb. The biggest government operation is Dobbins Air Force Base, located adjacent to Lockheed in Marietta. The base is large in area (1,665 acres) and in impact on the community. Its pilots log more than 100,000 "operations" per year, including takeoffs, landings, touch-and-gos, and other movements by aircraft. Most posts at the base are filled by reservists; if they all reported for duty simultaneously, the base's population would reach eight thousand.

A 1988 study fixed Dobbins's economic impact on the area within a fifty-mile radius at $132,675,985. The value of aircraft headquartered at Dobbins is $853.5 million.

But big is not the only way for business to go in Cobb. The county is, in fact, considered an "incubator" for small businesses, so much so that the *Wall Street Journal* says that Cobb is the country's small business capital. Why is Cobb so right for the small business? A favorable tax climate. Good highways and a sound infrastructure. Ample business parks and warehouses. Glamorous office parks. Plentiful retail shopping.

Cobb is a natural relocation and expansion location for both small businesses and national corpora-

tions, and the glue that holds the business community together is the Cobb Chamber of Commerce. Organized into six divisions (Cumberland, South Cobb, Marietta, East Cobb, Smyrna, and North Cobb) created along geographical lines, the Chamber has nearly five thousand members. Of those, more than 80 percent represent small businesses. More than two hundred are manufacturing firms, and another two hundred are international companies, one-third of which have their U.S. headquarters in the county.

One of the Chamber's goals for Cobb is a diversified economy; its overall mission is to support and improve the community's business environment. To achieve those ends, its efforts are organized into the following areas: economic and community development, governmental affairs, communications, and membership. New areas of focus include international economic development, small-business services, education, tourism, transportation, and division councils, to maintain closer ties to specific areas within the county.

The Chamber moved into new headquarters in 1984 debt free. Financier David Rockefeller donated the land for the building, and more than three hundred businesses and individuals donated $1.2 million to finance construction.

Economic development specialists at the Chamber can advise relocating and expanding businesses, with services that include site selection assistance and specific details of Cobb's economic advantages. The Small Business Services Department promotes entrepreneurship, offering direct help through seminars, counseling referrals, and networking opportunities, such as its Business-After-Hours gatherings. The department also highlights smaller firms during its Small Business Week activities and

serves an advocacy role for small businesses within the Chamber and in the public and private sectors.

The International Center is the Chamber's department charged with serving the area's substantial international business community. Its two main missions are international business development and increased community awareness and support of international business. Japan, the United Kingdom, Germany, and Canada are the foreign countries with the largest number of companies doing business in Cobb, but the list of countries with some business interest in the county reads almost like the contents of an atlas.

Export consultation and trade missions abroad to develop international investment opportunities and trade relationships are among the International Center's services. The center also maintains a library of resource publications for international business persons and sponsors seminars and informational forums. Publications produced by the center include a directory of international companies and a Family Orientation Guide available in several languages to incoming international families. The center is working with the county's school systems to translate essential forms and other documents into six languages. Worldfest, a celebration of international art, food, music, and other activities, originated by the International Center, has the potential to become a major festival.

Statistics are a valid measure of economic strength and potential growth. One good measure of the business climate is the health of the hospitality industry in an area. According to 1990 statistics from the Cobb-Marietta Convention and Visitors Bureau, the county offered 7,642 rooms in sixty-six hotels. The occupancy rate in those rooms is higher than the metro area's average. The hospitality industry itself ranks Cobb as one of the area's strongest hotel markets, and Cobb has one of the highest concentrations of all-suites hotels in the country.

The strength of the hospitality industry is also linked to the strength of tourism and travel in Cobb. Tourism is not just a historical fact. In 1989 travelers spent $647.6 million dollars in Cobb. Almost sixteen thousand jobs are supported in whole or in part by travelers, and tourism generated approximately $291 million in associated income. More than 50 percent of Cobb's visitors come from outside Georgia. Thousands also make day trips from close by to enjoy Six Flags or White Water, to shop, to attend the Bell-South Atlanta Classic golf tournament, to play softball or soccer, or to attend art and cultural events.

Another measure of the business environment is retail space. According to the *Atlanta Business Chronicle*, Cobb offers 14.5 million square feet of existing space; another 700,000 square feet are under construction, and 1.4 million square feet are planned. Major shopping areas, those with more than 200,000 square feet, include: Cumberland/ Galleria, the Marietta Trade Center, Akers Mill Square, Belmont Hills Shopping Center, Providence Square, Town & Country Plaza, Merchants Walk, and Parkaire Landing. Town Center, the newest regional mall, alone has one million square feet of retail space, and shopping centers surrounding the mall include six more with square footage in ex-

cess of 150,000.

The *Atlanta Business Chronicle* also cites Cobb County as one of the largest office submarkets in the Atlanta area. Eighteen million square feet of office space already exist. Another 1.1 million are under construction, and 2.7 million are on the drawing board. In 1974 Atlanta proper offered ten million square feet of office space; the northwest and north central areas, in comparison, had six million square feet. By 1984 Atlanta's space had increased to fourteen million square feet; the northwest and north central area's, to forty million. The shift happened largely because people

want their offices as close as possible
to their homes, and Cobb's excellent
proximity and access to Hartsfield
Airport means that moving a business to the suburbs doesn't mean
sacrificing the urban edge in competition and availability.

Nowhere is the county's future
more evident than in the Barrett development near Town Center mall.
Barrett is the largest mixed-use project in Cobb County. Begun in 1987,
its one thousand acres mix office,
hotel, retail, multi-family residential, and light industrial development. Barrett is a master-planned
community that can attract high-
quality residents, both business and
residential. Near McCollum Airport
for convenience, the development offers impressive landscaping in a natural urban setting in the shadow of
historic Kennesaw Mountain. Lakes,
parks, and extensive green areas dot
the landscape in accordance with a
minimum tree density requirement
throughout the complex. Maximum
development will allow only 40 percent of Barrett's land to be covered
by structures. Once complete, the
project will provide 100,000 jobs
and a full range of consumer and
business services.

But statistics can never tell the
whole story. Perhaps the best way to
understand just how healthy doing
business in Cobb can be is to hear to
the stories of some of its most successful companies. Listen:

BRENDA ROBERTS BRANCH

I have lived in Atlanta and its surrounding communities off and on for sixteen years. In May 1989 my husband and I purchased a home in Marietta.

As we searched for the ideal place, we wanted the best possible house for the money we had to invest. We also wanted to find a community in which our home would increase in value without risk of depreciation. Because I am basically a country girl at heart, we wanted a quiet, serene location that also gave us access to shopping centers, movie theaters, restaurants, and other features of urban living that we'd come to take for granted.

We wanted all this—and we wanted to be totally removed from the rat race that downtown Atlanta had become for us. It was hard to imagine, while we were looking, that our dream home could exist.

In the two years since we made our choice and moved to Cobb, I've seen constant improvements in an area that was outstanding enough to attract us originally. Cobb is getting even better. From the lawns in my neighborhood to the landscaping along the freeways and in office parks, for a flower lover like me, Cobb is indeed a beautiful place, brimming with an "I care" attitude.

Brenda Roberts Branch is Executive Vice President and Chief Operating Officer of Gourmet Services, Inc.

In 1988 Yvonnda "Susie" Piero founded her company, Y. S. Piero Designs, on a principle: a commitment to creativity and excellence in the art of floral design. Located on the Marietta Square, the company is much more than a flower shop.

In fact, one of Piero's strongest commitments is to providing the community with a distinctive gallery that displays a variety of art floral works, paintings, sculptures, and accessories.

Piero's commitment also extends beyond the business itself: She believes a business has an obligation to the community it serves. Thus, she is actively involved in a number of community issues and projects, bringing to them the same innovation and dedication that are trademarks of her company.

Piero's creative efforts and energies have already had considerable impact on the floral industry.

Peers and critics consider her intricate, creative designs innovative, challenging, and inspiring. In 1989 Piero was inducted into the American Institute of Floral Designers, and both

THE ART OF Y. S. PIERO DESIGNS & ASSOCIATES

the Metro Atlanta Floral Association and the Georgia State Floral Association have named her their Designer of the Year.

Piero's creative talents blend with equally strong business acumen. She has developed new product lines, price point programs, educational presentations, and innovative design panels for numerous companies—all to accomplish her goal of recognition

of professionalism within her industry. Working with interior designers and commercial and residential clients, Piero creates, produces, and markets unique floral concepts that clearly support her belief that floral design is a true artform.

A visit to Y. S. Piero Designs is an excursion into a world of beauty, where the unusual and unexpected combine to create the exceptional.

Piero and her associates, a team of involved artists who make crucial contributions to realizing Piero's vision, are gifted in all aspects of traditional, transitional, European, and contemporary design, and they work with the freshest available flowers from markets in Holland, South America, California, and Hawaii. The company also excels in producing the best and newest concepts in silk flower design and in alternative, cost-effective designs using balloons and flowers.

Adept at holiday and theme-oriented decoration, the company also serves weekly decorating needs for companies, businesses, and decorators; parties and banquets; bridal events and weddings; corporate functions; residential parties; grand openings; Bar/Bat Mitzvahs; and special client appreciation events.

At Y. S. Piero Designs the concept of integrating beauty—in stunning, innovative ways—with the total feel of a room or an event reaches new heights. Built on years of training and experience in floral design, the Piero concept looks ahead to the future as it transforms the industry today. Susie Piero's creativity in her art and in her business capture perfectly the spirit of success that defines Cobb County.

The Art of Y.S. Piero Designs & Associates

The origins of Barnett Bank of Atlanta lie deep in Cobb County's history. Founded in 1887 as the First National Bank of Marietta, the bank thrived for more than three-quarters of a century before being renamed the First National Bank of Cobb County in 1971. Two years later First National Bank of Cobb County merged with the Bank of Acworth.

Ninety-nine years after it first began to serve the citizens of Cobb County, the bank merged with Barnett Banks of Florida, Inc., the leading financial institution in the state of Florida. Less than one year after the merger, the newly formed Barnett Bank, N.A. had eleven offices in Cobb County and assets of $501 million. After merging

A 1989 merger with Investors Bank & Trust brought the number of offices to nineteen, spread across four counties; assets to $750 million. By the end of that year, two new offices

BARNETT BANK OF ATLANTA

had been opened and an additional twenty-six million dollars in assets acquired, making Barnett Bank of Atlanta the eighth-largest financial institution in Georgia.

Don D. Roberts was named presi-

Bank of Atlanta into the nineties, maintaining its long-standing ties to the community while pursuing a clear vision to ensure a successful and dynamic future.

Barnett is committed to adding value to its relationships with its customers through outstanding service and by providing financial services of the highest quality. Its corporate mission is to enhance its position as a preeminent banking organization in the Southeast and one of the leading banking organizations in the nation.

Still, Barnett Bank is aware that any plans for the future must be grounded in the basics. Thus, among the company's specific goals for the nineties are increased efficiency and

with First Fulton Bank & Trust in 1988, the company was renamed Barnett Bank of Atlanta. The new configuration included fifteen offices in Cobb and Fulton counties and $710 million in assets.

dent and chief executive officer of Barnett Bank of Atlanta in May 1990. Coming to Cobb County from almost two decades of distinguished banking experience in his native Texas and in Florida, Roberts will lead Barnett

improved customer service. This carefully poised balance of large-scale vision and attention to detail guarantees a second century of vital contributions to the life of Cobb County.

The site of the BellSouth Atlanta Classic is saturated with history and money. Sope Creek, which meanders through the course, was home to a Civil War-era paper mill that printed Confederate money. Its ruins are visible from the number-thirteen tee.

The Classic is connected to more recent history as well, for it has its beginnings in Cobb's mid-sixties boom. In 1964 Atlanta sportsman Jim Clay decided that Atlanta and professional golf were made for each other. He took his idea to every golf club in the city; every club turned it down.

So Clay and a half-dozen friends purchased hundreds of acres of farmland near the Chattahoochee River in Cobb County, built the Atlanta Country Club, and set out to court the PGA. To secure a PGA event, a nonprofit organization must be in place to provide financial underpinning. Clay and fifty or so friends put up a thousand dollars each to create the Atlanta Classic Foundation.

Then, according to the regulations of the day, the site hosted a two-day pro-am tournament to demonstrate its capabilities. The Atlanta "trial run" was a success, and in 1967 the Atlanta Golf Classic became

BELLSOUTH ATLANTA CLASSIC

part of the PGA Tour. Today, the event is one of the few on that tour to remain at its original site, which many competitors consider one of the tour's best. Today, more than 120,000 fans and millions more on television watch top pros compete for a purse that exceeds one million dollars.

Golf Digest ranks the course among the nation's hundred best. It plays to a par-72 and stretches more than seventy-one hundred yards. Originally designed by Willard Byrd,

the course has been enhanced by Joe Finger and Jack Nicklaus.

But a site alone doesn't make a tournament work. That takes people. To make the Classic a success, more than one thousand volunteers put in some twenty-eight thousand hours. Beginning in 1982, the business community joined the effort. Georgia-Pacific Corporation's title sponsorship made the Classic one of the first dozen tournaments on the tour to have such support. In 1989 BellSouth Corporation assumed this crucial role.

During the three years of BellSouth sponsorship, the tournament has donated nearly $1.5 million to Egleston Children's Hospital at Emory University.

Professional golf is unique in the sports world. No one owns the franchise. Thus, every PGA Tour event must have the support of both the business and golfing communities in the host city. The story of this event is a classic example of how that support happens in the best possible way.

In this increasingly complex world, many of us will need caring, professional treatment for mental-health problems. Brawner Psychiatric Institute has established itself as a leader in meeting these needs since its founding in 1910.

The treatment programs at Brawner–the true backbone of its success–continue to meet the needs of a rapidly changing society. There are distinct inpatient treatment programs for adult psychiatry, chemical dependency, and adolescents and young children. Alternative treatment services support each of these programs. In addition, a wide range of outpatient treatment services is available.

Each clinical program emphasizes individualized care, group and family therapy, and education–

BRAWNER PSYCHIATRIC INSTITUTE

children and adolescents attend Brookside School on campus.

Brawner's trained professionals offer state of the art mental health care, including psychological services, neuroendorocrine evaluations for clinical depression, comprehensive aftercare treatment planning, and family counseling. The hospital is licensed by the Georgia Department of Human Resources and fully accredited by the Joint Commission on Accreditation of Healthcare Organizations.

Tomorrow holds new and greater challenges for providing excellent and cost efficient mental health care. Brawner's physicians and staff are dedicated to meeting these challenges aggressively.

Brawner Psychiatric Institute

The centerpiece of northwest Atlanta, the Galleria is the premier location for today's business leaders. The Galleria's elegance and exceptional quality have long been recognized by leading corporate names world-wide. Tenants include numerous Fortune 500 companies as well as Atlanta's most prestigious financial institutions, law and accounting firms, and other professional organizations.

Conceived in 1978, the Galleria is Atlanta's most comprehensive business environment. Surrounded by the award-winning Galleria gardens, the office towers combine classic architecture and state-of-the-art technology. The four-star Stouffer Waverly Hotel provides guests with world-class accommodations, and the fashionable Galleria Specialty Mall offers shopping at more than sixty stores and many

round musical and theatrical performances, exhibits, and events, the Galleria creates a delightful atmosphere for both business and pleasure.

CHILDRESS
KLEIN
PROPERTIES
—
ATLANTA
GALLERIA

The Galleria offers its executive community Atlanta's most complete assortment of amenities, among them the luxury of private club dining, professional child care, and the convenience of the Stouffer Waverly's superb meeting and convention facilities. Tenants can exercise in the athletic club or take a lunchtime jog

destinations with their own reputation, offering concerts in the park at lunchtime and many evening and weekend events from international festivals to community-related activities.

Childress Klein Properties' management staff can best be summarized in one word—responsive. More than an attitude, this is a commitment shared by a team of attentive professionals thoroughly trained in every aspect of property management—engineering, landscaping, accounting, tenant finish supervision, building systems, life safety and security. Childress Klein Properties is committed to meeting the changing needs of the Galleria tenant community and to preserving a long-standing reputation for quality and service.

Ultimately, the quality of an office development enhances a company's

fine restaurants.

Innovation, quality, and service are the cornerstones of the Galleria's reputation. Transcending the traditional idea that an office development is for business only, the Galleria has established itself as a cultural and entertainment center. Home to year-

around the running track, as well as handle personal banking or dry cleaning. A broad variety of personal services—from an executive car wash to a haircut and shoeshine—can be found within the complex.

The lush park and gardens and natural amphitheater have become

image. The work environment contributes significantly to the enjoyment and productivity of its employees and, thus, to the success of its business. No finer atmosphere exists for meeting these objectives than at the Atlanta Galleria: the continuing standard of excellence.

Marietta is metro Atlanta's third largest city, with a population of more than forty-three thousand. A highly visible part of the area's vibrant growth, Marietta is also still small enough to provide the sense of genuine community that most people seek.

The city's newly established Development and Planning Department is committed to shaping Marietta's growth in ways that will honor the past while ensuring a prosperous future. The department's mission involves strategic planning for development and aggressive marketing of the community's high quality of life. Marietta is dedicated to being a responsible steward of its heritage and assets, to maintaining an economically balanced, diverse community.

The city provides services unparalleled in the metropolitan area; in fact, few communities in the nation serve their citizens so well. For example, Marietta Power, which provides electrical and other services to more than forty-one thousand customers in the city and actively competes for business within the entire Cobb County area, is a totally nonprofit organization. All revenues generated by Marietta Power go directly back into the city—for services and development.

CITY OF MARIETTA
MARIETTA POWER

This unique relationship creates a number of advantages for Mariettans, among them taxes that are the lowest in the metro area. The city's 1989-90 tax millage rate remained lower than the rate levied in 1960. And this in the same year that saw Marietta Power's rates *reduced* approximately 6 percent!

But low taxes and decreased utility rates don't mean diminished services. Marietta's independent school system, already the envy of many communities, will be even stronger thanks to improvements funded by a $20.8 million bond referendum. The computer labs now in all city schools can be equalled by fewer than a half-dozen systems nationwide.

Marietta police respond faster than the national average. The city's sprinkling ordinance has made it a model for fire prevention. In Marietta, garbage pick-up happens in backyards, not at the curb. The city's seventeen parks have recently been expanded to include the Old Marietta Country Club. After a two-million-dollar refurbishing, the club will open as Cobb County's first public PGA standard golf course.

The people who power Marietta—the employees of the city and Marietta Power—have played a major role in the preservation of the enviable quality of life Mariettans now enjoy. And they are committed to the principle they have followed for more than 150 years—people serving people.

The Platinum Triangle sits not far from Standing Peachtree, Cobb's cradle of commerce, where today's residents are again making history through the Cobb County Community Improvement District.

Since 1975 the area stretching from Vinings in the south beyond Powers Ferry Road to the north has seen more than fourteen million square feet of office space constructed, with matching growth in retail and hospitality facilities. More than sixty thousand people come daily to work, shop, and entertain themselves and clients. Projections indicate that the present density could increase by 150 percent.

Community Improvement District, the first in the Southeast, was created. At the request of the Cobb Chamber of Commerce and the Cobb County Board of Commissioners, in 1988 the

COBB COUNTY COMMUNITY IMPROVEMENT DISTRICT

Georgia General Assembly authorized the creation of self-taxing districts. The funds for improvements within defined geographic areas could

property tax rate of five mills produces annual revenues of $2.2 million, all solely for transportation improvements within the District.

Now a viable economic force, the District works on issues and concerns affecting property owners and visitors to its area. Combining immediate pragmatic concerns with a visionary approach to the future, the District has the potential to become a model for the entire country. This unique example of businesses agreeing to extra taxes to leverage immediate improvements in their arena signals the sort of public-private partnership that is the key to future growth that respects and preserves a com-

Such growth inevitably brings infrastructure needs that outstrip the resources of government and stretch the limits of conventional remedies. Self-evident solutions are usually hard to define and implement. Thus, history must be made.

And that is exactly why the

be raised if property owners decided to assess themselves additional taxes.

By May 1988 business leaders in the Platinum Triangle had garnered support from enough commercial property owners to implement the improvement district plan in their area. The additional commercial

munity's quality of life.

Perhaps no single organization better exemplifies the innovative strength of Cobb County than its Community Improvement District—business and government working together to make Cobb the best place to live and work.

Reporting on the 1965 ground-breaking ceremony for "Cobb Memorial Hospital," the Atlanta newspapers called the location "a peripheral area of Cobb County." But the *Cobb County Times* proved more prophetic, calling the groundbreaking "a milestone in the history of Cobb County."

Cobb General Hospital opened its doors on June 3, 1968. Its medical-dental staff numbered fifty-eight, and its 167 beds were attended by 150 full-time and thirty part-time employees. The first year also saw seventy-five adult volunteers and ninety Candy Stripers put in nearly twelve thousand hours of service. From the beginning, Cobb General was truly a community endeavor.

Today, a number of programs and events demonstrate the hospital's integral role in community life. Cobb General began the nineties by changing its name to reflect more accurately its evolving role. Cobb General became Cobb Hospital & Medical Center, a name befitting its efforts on behalf of the community's overall good health.

In addition to increased technology such as magnetic resonance imaging, laser treatment, and cardiac catheterization, Cobb Hospital & Medical Center offers such innovations as Kids' Corner, an afterhours pediatric treatment facility, a Family Education Series of year-round wellness classes, and Senior Health Plus, a club to ensure ongoing good health for those fifty-five and older. In its rehabilitation unit CHMC offers new hope for those facing disabling illnesses or injuries. Both patients and family learn new ways to deal with and compensate for disabilities in this program aimed at helping every patient attain the maximum independence

and quality of life possible for him or her.

In May 1990, CHMC became a trauma triage center as part of the District III Trauma Network. The hospital

COBB HOSPITAL & MEDICAL CENTER

has always been involved in managing trauma, but this official designation by the Regional Emergency Management System recognizes the program's excellence and gives CHMC expanded access to other trauma centers.

And Cobb Hospital & Medical Center's involvement doesn't stop at

Cobb Hospital & Medical Center

their doors. Each May CHMC sponsors a 5K road race to benefit their Cancer Support Service. August finds two thousand people of all ages on the Center's lawn for the Candlelite Concert Series of the South Cobb Arts Alliance and the South Cobb Improvement Association. In December the Love Light Tree glows with donations

in honor or memory of special friends; proceeds help equip the hospital.

Cobb Hospital and Medical Center proudly serves Still and Dowell elementary schools and Garrett Middle School in the Partners in Education program, participating in a number of special events and projects with the student bodies of each school. For those beyond school age, the Center sponsors a walking program to help citizens stay fit.

A Speakers Bureau sends educated professionals out into the community to share time and expertise. Kirby the Chipmunk, mascot of Kids' Corner, entertains and instructs children's groups throughout the county, and each Halloween the Center provides a free candy-screening service in the Diagnostic Center. Lifeline, a personal emergency response system, allows senior citizens to maintain their independence through electronic connection to CHMC. The Wellness Alliance promotes community and industrial health education through classes, many at no charge. Screenings for various health concerns are taken out into the community on a regular basis.

In short, Cobb Hospital & Medical Center weaves itself throughout the fabric of life in Cobb County, making the community stronger, healthier, and happier. And the community has woven itself into the fabric of the hospital, too. Its volunteer arm, the Cobb Hospital & Medical Center Auxiliary, in the hospital's first twenty years, contributed more than a half-million service hours, $612,710, and twenty-eight nursing scholarships.

Cobb Hospital & Medical Center has always prided itself on being a leader in its field. To meet the needs of Cobb's burgeoning business environment, they developed the CHV Occupational Health Care program, which offers businesses a full range of employee physical screenings, workers' compensation coordination, and convenient treatment for minor illnesses and injuries at low cost with minimal waiting.

Cobb Hospital & Medical Center has turned its less-than-humble dreams into a reality, serving one of the nation's most rapidly growing areas as a 333-bed multi-service hospital and comprehensive medical center with more than two hundred

Cobb Hospital & Medical Center

physicians, every major medical specialty, state-of-the-art technology, unparalleled intensive care and cardiac intensive care units, and many of tomorrow's necessities already in working order today.

Best of all, growth and expansion haven't destroyed the real strength of Cobb Hospital & Medical Center. The warm, personal treatment their patients have come to expect is still top priority. At CHMC people have always come first and always will.

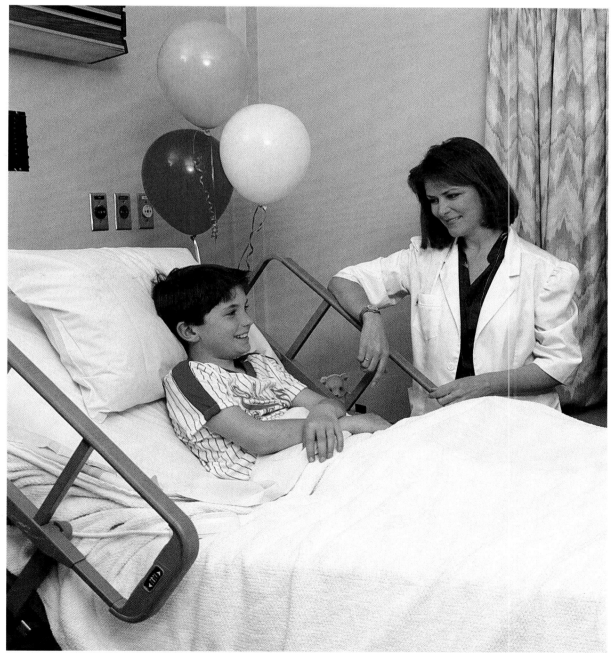

In December 1938 Senator Richard B. Russell pulled a switch that first sent electricity to 489 farm members and fourteen commercial accounts of the Cobb Electric Membership Corporation.

Now 100,000 members strong, Cobb EMC is the largest of Georgia's EMCs and the fourth largest EMC in the nation. A nonprofit, member-owned corporation, governed by a nine-member board of directors elected from the membership, it is dedicated to providing its member-owners with the best service at the lowest possible price. More than 450 dedicated employees, including an engineering staff with more than two hundred years of combined experience, serve an area covering approximately 415 square miles, transversed by more than fifty-five hundred miles of line.

In 1990 Cobb EMC sold 1.6 billion kilowatt hours of electricity, generating revenues exceeding $128.5 million.

On the environmental front Cobb EMC offers its Good Cents program, an energy-efficient construction package; low-interest loans for energy-efficient home improvements; and complimentary technical advice on energy conservation. It was the first utility in the nation to launch a system-wide volunteer load-management program, utilizing radio-controlled switches to cycle off air conditioners.

This peak-demand-reduction program saved members $225,000 in 1976, its initial year. As of 1990, the program has lowered Cobb EMC's wholesale power costs by some $25

COBB ELECTRIC MEMBERSHIP CORPORATION

million. The company has also initiated an in-house recycling program.

Community service areas include funding of the Foster Kid Camp for

All monies for Cobb EMC's community service programs come not from the sale of electricity but from the in-house recycling program and the rental receipts from a billboard on the company's property.

The Women's Task Force, established in 1976, is another good example of the way Cobb EMC reaches out to serve its community. The volunteer task force funds a local high-school student's participation in a nationally organized youth tour of Washington, DC, and in recent years has also provided college scholarship funds to local students.

True to its roots in the effort to enhance lives through rural electrifica-

Cobb Electric Membership Corporation

Cobb and Cherokee counties; the Cobb Department of Family and Children Services' Adult Protective Services Program; the YWCA Battered Women's Shelter; and a Teen Shelter for troubled youth.

tion, Cobb EMC continues to operate by the philosophy that its job is to assist in bringing the best quality of life to its members and its community.

Cobb Electric Membership Corporation

Cousins Properties Incorporated, a publicly owned, diversified real estate development company, was founded in 1958 by I. W. Cousins and his son, Thomas G. Cousins, now Chairman of the Board and President. The company is dedicated to creating outstanding values in real estate and can lay claim to having built more than 9.25 million square feet of office space, ten million square feet of retail space, including ten regional malls, three thousand multi-family residential units, and fifteen prestigious family subdivisions.

In 1983 the company decided to concentrate its efforts on high-quality office projects, and perhaps nowhere are the fruits of that decision more evident than in Wildwood Office Park in eastern Cobb County. A joint venture between Cousins Properties Incorporated and the IBM Corporation, Wildwood's centerpiece is the Wildwood Plaza building, designed

tively when they are continually nurtured by the natural environment. Wildwood is one of the country's most desirable sites for a commercial office park—289 wooded acres, overlooking

COUSINS PROPERTIES
WILDWOOD OFFICE PARK

Atlanta and Cobb County and bounded by twelve hundred acres of the Chattahoochee National Forest.

When Pei first saw the site for Wildwood Plaza, his reaction was that the property was "the most beautiful site I've worked on." His recommendation was a masterplan emphasizing "a series of strong elements separated by areas of light development." In keeping with that idea, Pei, the architect for the John F. Kennedy Library,

story twin-tower office building. The towers, of polished granite and pewter glass to reflect their environment, will be joined by a lobby enclosed by a sixty-foot-high glass pyramid roof. A 130-foot diameter fountain will adorn the building's front.

The international stature Pei brings to the project enhances the architectural reputation of the entire area. Wildwood has already reaped a series of awards, including the Associated Landscape Contractors of America's Environmental Improvement Grand Award, given for "efforts in improving the environment for the benefit of mankind and for promoting, protecting, and preserving the heritage of beauty for all future generations."

Due for completion in April 1991, Pei's masterful Wildwood Plaza will join four other completed, award-winning buildings--2300, 3301, and 2500 Windy Ridge Parkway and 3100 Windy Hill Road—as the corner-

©Gordon Kilgore

by renowned architect I. M. Pei.

The guiding concept behind Wildwood is the conviction that people work more creatively and produc-

the East Wing of the National Gallery of Art, and the glass pyramid addition to the Grand Louvre in Paris, designed a 757,200-square-foot, fifteen-

stones of Cobb County's premier office park, where nature and architectural genius combine to create an ideal work environment.

Confederation Life is an excellent example of Cobb County's increasingly international business community. When the Canadian company made the decision to open a U.S. headquarters, a search for a suitable city led them to Atlanta. A subsequent search for a site within metro Atlanta brought Confederation Life to Cobb's Interstate North Office Park.

For five years the company rented space there while its new U.S. headquarters building was constructed on the sixteen-plus-acre site they had purchased in the park. Fifty-five Canadian families made the move to Cobb. Today, Confederation Life is comfortably settled in 266,000 square feet of Cobb County space, and provides employment for some 850 persons.

For more than a century Confederation Life has served those who

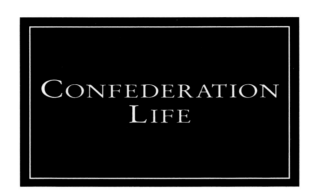

choice, making Confederation Life the fastest-growing of Canada's major life insurance companies, and the nineteenth-largest insurance company in the U.S. as measured by

assets under management. These assets currently exceed twenty billion dollars.

In addition to the traditional services provided by a mutual insurance company, Confederation Life, through its subsidiary Confed Admin Services Inc., provides a full range of benefits administration, managed healthcare, data reporting, and analysis services to

obligation, Confederation Life defines quality simply: quality is excellence in meeting their customers' needs.

Certain philosophical touchstones guarantee that excellence: The integrity that comes from fulfilling promises, being honest, speaking and acting with consistency, adhering to the highest possible ethical standards.

The empathy that grows out of a caring, sensitive, and courteous attitude firmly rooted in knowledge and understanding of customers.

The effective communication that opens the exchange of information between company and customer.

The competitiveness that springs from responsiveness to the marketplace, efficient use of resources, and providing excellent value.

The accuracy and timeliness that are the hallmarks of any successful enterprise.

Confederation Life

depend on them, providing its customers with confidence in their futures and in their children's futures. When a customer chooses Confederation Life, he or she is choosing quality and service.

Thousands have made that

self-insured corporations throughout the U.S.

Life insurance is, in large measure, a representation of stability and tradition within a framework of progress and exciting growth. To ensure that its performance fulfills that

A member of the elite few in the insurance industry given the highest possible ratings by industry analysts and experts, Confederation Life is able to provide international service with a genuine personal touch, making them a perfect match with their U.S. home.

Ernest Barrett, an active participant in so much of Cobb County's development, was there when The Georgian Club opened in 1983, toasting the county's first city club, and one of the country's first suburban city clubs. Since that auspicious occasion, The Georgian Club has played host to the area's most influential and successful citizens, as well as to many distinguished visitors, ranging from actor Paul Newman and news anchor Peter Jennings to former president Jimmy Carter and Elizabeth Dole, director of the American Red Cross.

Located on the seventeenth floor

George II interior. The club's exclusive approach to service reflects a solid respect for tradition and an appropriate awareness of contemporary business and social entertainment

THE GEORGIAN CLUB
INDIAN HILLS COUNTRY CLUB

needs. Equipped to accommodate a variety of meeting and dining needs, in addition to offering nightly enter-

southern traditional cuisines in an unparalleled atmosphere.

During the business day or when the work week is done, Indian Hills Country Club in East Cobb stands ready to meet the discerning member's leisure and recreational needs. Twenty-seven holes of challenging golf, ten tennis courts, two pools, and a flurry of social activities make Indian Hills Country Club the ideal spot for business or relaxing.

The main dining room and the Men's Grill, as well as a poolside snack bar in summer and year-round private dining rooms, offer members the ideal dining experience for any occasion, formal or casual.

Founded in 1969, Indian Hills Country Club has opened its third decade with an ambitious master plan for upgrading and enhancing its grounds and facilities. This goal of making a good thing even better reflects Indian Hills Country Club's commitment to the highest standards of service to its members and to their families and guests.

Whether it's an elegant business setting or a challenging game of golf that Cobb's leaders need, The Georgian Club and Indian Hills Country Club have everything necessary for world-class entertainment, meetings, and play.

©Fred S. Gerlich

of 100 Galleria Tower, the club offers a spectacular view, rivaled in beauty only by its tasteful, inviting King

tainment and special activities' services, The Georgian Club offers the best of continental, American, and

©David Clarke

Founded in 1970 by Parker H. ("Pete") Petit, Healthdyne, Inc., boasted 1990 revenues of $138 million and an after-tax profit of eight million dollars for its three divisions: Home Nutritional Services, the nation's third-largest supplier of home intravenous therapy; Healthdyne Perinatal Services, the country's second-largest provider of home obstetrical care; and Healthdyne Technologies, a manufacturer of high-tech home-healthcare equipment distributed in the United States and abroad. Together, these divisions employ more than two thousand people.

But such object facts don't do the Healthdyne story justice.

In 1964 Pete Petit left Georgia Institute of Technology with degrees in mechanical engineering and engineering mechanics. After serving with a U.S. Army aviation unit, he worked in the aviation industry, first for General Dynamics, then for Lockheed, returning to his native Atlanta.

As the seventies dawned, Petit found himself longing for a greater professional challenge. He'd always worked for others, but suddenly entrepreneurial fever hit. In that same year tragedy also struck. Petit lost a son to crib death, now known as SIDS

(Sudden Infant Death Syndrome). Out of grief and the desire to shape his own professional destiny, Petit carved the business that has become one of Cobb County's strongest international

HEALTHDYNE, INCORPORATED

corporations.

Using his considerable engineering training to transform loss into something positive and lasting, Petit formulated a design for equipment that could monitor an infant's breathing and heart activity in a home setting. He shared his idea with the physician who had treated his late son. The doctor saw its potential for sparing other families the agony the Petits had suffered.

But in the early seventies there was little financial or other meaningful support for fledgling technical ventures, especially in the Southeast. Petit forged ahead anyway, calling on a former roommate who had become an electrical engineer. That contact led to others that eventually gave Petit access to Georgia Tech labs on weekends and in the evenings.

Several physicians invested in Petit's idea, but capital remained dangerously low in the early years. Products were developed, but the means to market them didn't exist. Finally, a loan from the Small Business Administration and new capital from Henry Curtis, chairman and CEO of American Business Products, and from a second mortgage on Petit's home turned things around. In addition, Petit had become a more astute businessman through earning an

MBA in finance by attending night classes at Georgia State University.

Thus, the story of Healthdyne's origins, growth, and eventual amazing success is a story of loss transformed, of a man's personal growth, his movement away from the safe, conservative world of cashing his paycheck from somebody else's company to the riskier but ultimately more rewarding world of forming his own company and making it work.

Of the three divisions that make up Healthdyne, only Home Nutritional Support is publicly traded as a separate entity, with Healthdyne owning 67 percent

of the stock. Healthdyne Perinatal Services and Healthdyne Technologies are wholly owned subsidiaries.

Home Nutritional Support offers nutritional, antibiotic, and chemotherapy infusion support to a variety of homebound patients through pharmacists and nurses at thirty service centers across the country. As the healthcare industry as a whole moves in the direction of more home-based care, Home Nutritional Support, as a successful model, establishes Healthdyne as a trendsetter for the industry as a whole.

Healthdyne Perinatal Services provides the "System 37" home

uterine activity monitor, which permits women at risk of experiencing early labor to stay at home or to continue working while uterine contraction activity is monitored twice a day and telecommunicated to one of Healthdyne's twenty-eight perinatal centers. The division offers a similar program for pregnant women at risk because of hypertension.

And Healthdyne Technologies manufactures and markets home-care products that address or monitor respiratory diseases, sleep disorders, high-risk pregnancies, and SIDS, all in the home setting.

Just as Healthdyne's origins lay in personal experience, Pete Petit continues to have an active personal involvement not only with the business he began two decades ago but also with the issues that inspired him. He has endowed a chair of Engineering in Medicine at Georgia Tech and serves on the National Council for Medicine at the Emory University School of Medicine and the Council for the Emory-Georgia Tech Biomedical Research Center. All of his six children

have grown up with Healthdyne, its successes and failures, as part of the family dialogue. Petit believes in learning from the lessons life hands us and sharing that knowledge with others.

The board chairman of the SIDS Alliance and a board member of the SIDS Foundation, Petit remains frustrated at the lack of progress in SIDS research. His personal success notwithstanding, he chose to become active in these national organizations because not enough has been done to spare other families.

Healthdyne is considered a model of how to make sophisticated home healthcare a reality. Pete Petit is a model of how to turn personal loss and frustration into positive professional and social action, the epitome of entrepreneurialism at its best.

Healthdyne, Incorporated

Healthdyne, Incorporated

Thomas R. Egleston had a dream: "To treat sick children, to encourage scientific investigation into medical problems of children, and to provide instruction in the disease and care of children." In 1916 his generous bequest laid the foundation for making that dream a reality. His mother, Henrietta Holmes Egleston, lost four of her five children in early childhood. Her surviving son was determined that other mothers would not suffer such tragedy.

Today, Egleston is the largest and most comprehensive children's medical center in Georgia, and has the distinction of being the only university-based, free-standing children's hospital in the state. A 235-licensed-bed referral hospital, Egleston is involved in the diagnosis, treatment and research of childhood diseases and life-threatening illnesses and injuries.

The Children's Heart Center is one of the country's largest cardiology and cardiovascular surgery programs for children. Egleston's childhood cancer program is one of the country's largest. Other services include heart,

heart-lung, kidney, liver, corneal, and bone marrow transplants and Georgia's only pediatric kidney dialysis unit.

As a designated pediatric trauma

EGLESTON CHILDREN'S HOSPITAL

center, Egleston is well-equipped to handle all types of trauma twenty-four hours a day. The hospital also houses one of only five university-affiliated children's medical-psychiatric units in the country.

In 1959 Egleston moved from its original location to the Emory University campus to become the on-campus clinical site for pediatric education, and the hospital is affiliated with the Robert W. Woodruff Health Sciences Center of the Emory University School of Medicine. In addition to education, the move to Emory was also planned so that

research could be conducted. And in 1985 the Emory-Egleston Children's Research Center was formed, combining the expertise of the Emory investigators with Egleston's strong commitment to improving the quality of children's lives.

Seventy-three thousand young patients each year, from throughout Georgia, across the nation, and several foreign countries come to Egleston for in and out-patient treatment. The patients and their families are cared for by a team specially trained and

Egleston Children's Hospital

prepared to serve the unique needs of children.

Egleston's commitment to Georgia's children is recognized and generously supported by the community. More than nine hundred volunteers provide more than fifty thousand hours of service each year. Thirty-seven neighborhood groups known as Twigs, and individuals in the hospital auxiliary, represent almost three-thousand members throughout the metropolitan area who support the children. In 1989 alone these groups raised $1.4 million for Egleston. Among the community events that support the hospital are the BellSouth Atlanta Classic and the annual Festival of Trees. Egleston and the community it serves are united and committed to continuing the realization of Thomas Egleston's dream.

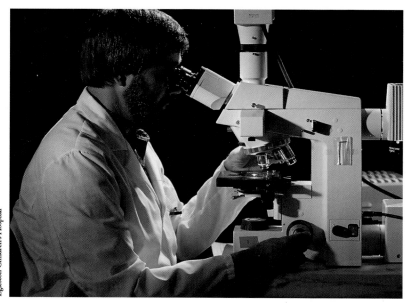
Egleston Children's Hospital

Kennestone Hospital opened in 1950, with sixty beds and a staff of fifty-two, serving a quieter, simpler Cobb County. But the dynamic forces that reshaped the county have also reshaped Kennestone. The small-town hospital is now Georgia's second-largest healthcare system. Six hundred physicians, five hundred volunteers, and a staff of more than three thousand serve more than 100,000 patients annually.

Between them, Kennestone Hospital in Marietta and Kennestone Hospital at Windy Hill have 654 beds; host forty-five hundred births; offer health education and corporate health programs that take the Kennestone philosophy back out into the community.

That philosophy was articulated by a Kennestone nurse and has become the system's theme: "Professionally we serve, personally we care." Although Kennestone now has high technology and advanced diagnostic and treatment capability, the personal attention and warm, compassionate attitude that we associate with the system's early days is still the essence of the Kennestone System.

From minor emergencies to major surgery, Kennestone stands ready to meet Cobb's healthcare needs. The Maternity Center allows the whole family to participate in births. Outpatient surgery centers provide an efficient, cost-effective approach to high-quality surgical care. For the heart: a Cardiac Catherization Laboratory, progressive Coronary Care Unit, Cardiac Rehabilitation. A Cancer Center. A Trauma Center. Mental health services. An Advanced Diagnostic Imaging Center. This is Kennestone.

A state-designated trauma center, Kennestone Marietta's Emergency Center is one of the state's busiest. Dr. David Tucker, head of the Metro Atlanta Trauma Network, says, "Ask other trauma surgeons or emergency room technicians where they would

KENNESTONE REGIONAL HEALTH CARE SYSTEM

like to be taken if critically injured, and most would say Kennestone."

For minor illnesses and injuries, KennMed Neighborhood Health Care Centers promise quick, neighborly attention. Special departments attend to women's health concerns. Atherton Place, on the Kennestone Marietta campus, features efficiencies and apartments and a broad range of services and activities for senior citizens. Health Place, Kennestone's fitness and wellness center, also on the Marietta campus, has as its motto, "We take every body seriously." An extensive corporate health program focuses on the unique healthcare needs of local businesses: employee physicals, health education classes, corporate fitness programs, drug testing, EAPs and worker's compensation treatment.

Supported by the Kennestone Foundation, with its board of more than one hundred community leaders, and by hundreds of dedicated volunteers, Kennestone is dedicated to serving the Cobb community professionally and personally.

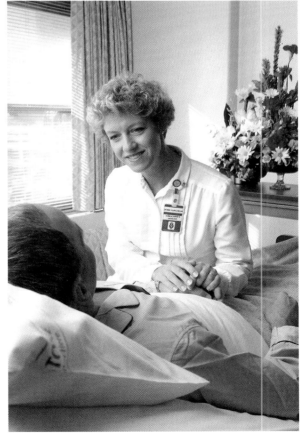

© Glenn Bewley, Atlanta

The history of the Lockheed Aeronautical Systems Company reflects the history of the United States in the twentieth-century.

Lockheed began to take shape in 1913 when two brothers— not the famous Wrights of Ohio and Kitty Hawk, but Allan and Malcolm Loughead (pronounced Lockheed; hence, the company's name)—successfully flew their first hand-built three-passenger seaplane. Three years later they founded a company in Santa Barbara, California, to manufacture a twin-engine ten-passenger flying boat, two seaplanes for the Navy (thus establishing an important link to the military), and a small biplane.

A glut of surplus World War I planes hurt the aviation entrepeneurs, who folded their company. Malcolm went on to other pursuits, including inventing the Lockheed four-wheel hydraulic brake system for cars. But Allan was not cured of aviation fever. He opened Lockheed Aircraft Company in Hollywood in 1926.

Purchased in 1929 by Detroit Aircraft, the thriving firm went into receivership with its parent company after the stock market crash later that year. A group headed by Robert E. Gross bought Lockheed's assets for forty thousand dollars in 1932. In 1934 the company's first Model 10 Electra took off; so did its fortunes. For the next fifteen years civilian and military planes poured off Lockheed assembly lines, including twenty thousand planes used in World War II.

The Marietta facility was built by Bell Aircraft during thirteen months at the beginning of WWII to turn out B-29 bombers. Production shut down after VJ Day, but in 1951 the government asked Lockheed to reopen the facility to modify B-29 aircraft for the conflict in Korea. The plant has re-

mained open since then.

The original focus of the Marietta facility on B-29s was expanded to include first B-47s and then C-130 Hercules aircraft. In 1956 an

LOCKHEED AERONAUTICAL SYSTEMS COMPANY

Australian order for twelve of the Hercules planes opened the foreign market to Lockheed. The sixties saw the first JetStar, an executive jet, take off. Though this plane never became a military standard, government and corporate orders ensured its success.

All of these planes were designed and constructed as models elsewhere before being put into mass production in Marietta. The C-141, the StarLifter, contracted for in 1961, marked the debut of Lockheed-Georgia's concept-to-flyaway program. The StarLifter's first flight was on December 17, 1963, the sixtieth anniversary of the Wright brothers' first powered flight. In September 1965 Lockheed was awarded a U.S. Air Force Contract to build the C-5A, the free world's largest aircraft. The first C-5A lifted off the Dobbins runway on June 30, 1968.

The Hercules remains the most popular airfreighter in aviation history, having amassed more than sixteen million flight hours in sixty countries and having generated gross sales of more than $7.7 billion. The C-5 holds U.S. records of a different sort: it has flown 922,000 pounds, the greatest recorded weight flown by any U.S. aircraft, and it has also lifted a payload of 232,477 pounds to a record altitude of two thousand meters.

High technology and research

and development are very much a part of Lockheed's future. In 1988 the company's work on metal matrix composites was cited as one of the one hundred most significant products worldwide. That same year Georgia's Water and Pollution Control Association awarded the company the Outstanding Laboratory Award for its advances in pollution abatement.

The company employs more than ten thousand people, almost half residents of Cobb County. The weekly payroll runs $7.9 million, and Lockheed's tax bill comes to $36 million. In 1989 the company spent more than $84 million on goods and services from almost three thousand Georgia businesses. Since 1951 more than $2.2 billion Lockheed dollars have been pumped into the local economy through awards to Georgia firms.

But bigness is not measured in dollars and acres alone. Lockheed has a notoriously big heart as well. In December 1984 employees set a state record by donating 1,409 pints of blood, then collected forty-five thousand pounds of food for more than six hundred area underprivileged families. When employees of Lockheed's feeder plant in Charleston, South Carolina, were reeling from Hurricane Hugo's devastation, their Marietta peers responded with six tractor-trailer loads of food and supplies and five thousand gallons of gasoline.

The county's largest single employer, Lockheed further strengthened its ties to this area in 1989, when it moved the Lockheed Aeronautical Systems' company headquarters from California to Marietta. In 1991 Lockheed won the $90 billion Advanced Technical Fighter Program. Lockheed is immersed in and permeates every facet of life in Cobb, working and caring with unparalleled largeness.

In 1944 company chairman Akira Murata recognized the ever-increasing demand for electronic components as a sterling business opportunity and founded Murata Manufacturing Company, Ltd., to meet that demand. From its inception Murata Manufacturing Company, Ltd., has been a company dedicated to the manufacture of state-of-the-art ceramic capacitors. Ongoing expansion of its research and manufacturing capabilities enabled the company to establish itself as one of the world's foremost purveyors of electronic components by the early 1960s. By the mid-sixties Murata Corporation of America, a wholly owned subsidiary of Murata Manufacturing Company, Ltd., of Kyoto, Japan, was formed to take advantage of the strong demand for Murata's product in North America.

Erie Technological Products, Inc., was founded in Erie, Pennsylvania, in 1928. Its original name, Erie Resistor Corporation, reflects its earliest mission: the manufacture of high-quality resistor products. Over the years the company extensively broadened its product line through both internal expansion and acquisitions. Its well-known lines of ceramic capacitors, EMI/RFI filters, and crystal products made Erie Technological Products, Inc., a natural and attractive partner for Murata Manufacturing Company, Ltd. ETP's strong North American manufacturing and distribution facilities were key to expanding Murata Manufacturing Company's North American interests.

The origins of Murata Erie North America, Inc., extend as far back in time as 1928 and as far away in geography as Japan. In March 1981 the extremely successful U.S. marketing arm of Murata Manufacturing Company, Ltd., of Kyoto, Japan, merged with Erie Technological Products, Inc., an established U.S. manufacturer of electronic components, to form the newly identified corporation of Murata Erie North America, Inc.

MURATA ERIE NORTH AMERICA

The corporate headquarters of the newly formed company was established in Marietta and later moved to Smyrna, making Cobb County the hub of activity for the North American marketplace. In addition to the Smyrna headquarters, the firm's North American operations are located in State College, Pennsylvania; Rockmart, Georgia; and Trenton, Ontario, Canada.

Today, Murata Erie is committed to producing reliable, high-quality electronic components. Continuing emphasis on research and develop-

Murata-Erie North America

ment and the interrelated technologies of ceramics, metal engineering, electronics, electrochemistry, and electro-mechanics, combined with superior production and marketing of the resulting products, defines Murata Erie's strategy for meeting today's challenges and preparing to grow exponentially in order to meet tomorrow's demands.

In December 1985 Murata Erie occupied its new, modern facility in Smyrna. The thirty-thousand-square-foot corporate headquarters embodies the latest in architectural and building features, providing an exciting atmosphere, which contributes to staff productivity.

The Smyrna office includes a highly automated sales and engineering service center. Products offered through the Smyrna facility include: piezo alarms, ceramic filters, trimming potentiometers, resistor networks, surface mounted devices, posistors, flyback transformers, and focus adjusting resistors. Murata Erie's goal is to provide customers with an unsurpassed selection of electronic components suited to their individual design requirements.

One of Murata Erie's slogans is "Innovatively Integrating Technologies," but in reality the company is an innovator in other integrations just as significant. Drawing on the strengths of two businesses and two cultures, the company has assembled an enterprise that is a model of tomorrow in the competitive field of high-tech manufacturing.

Thus, Murata Erie represents an important trend in American business, with its dedication to old-fashioned value and service and its forward-looking commitment to strong international ties in order to bring its customers the best in modern technology and product development.

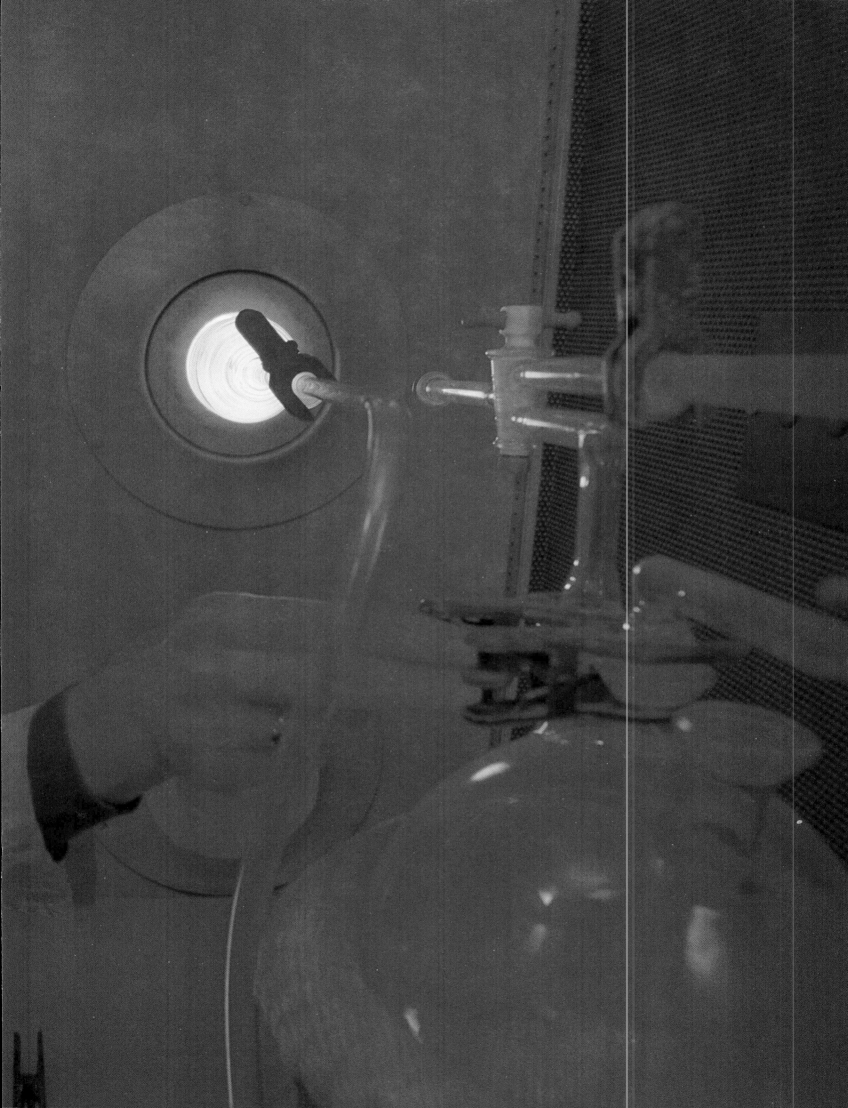

Today, Post Properties' communities comprise 25 percent of metropolitan Atlanta's upscale multifamily housing market, making Post one of Georgia's largest developers. In addition, the company has branched out with developments in Florida and Virginia.

But in 1971 John Williams, the entrepreneurial genius behind the Post legend, held his business meetings at the Sandy Springs International House of Pancakes, taking over a table to meet with prospective investors. He had a vision and twenty-five thousand dollars.

Today he oversees a network of more than fifteen thousand apartment homes in approximately fifty Post communities. His umbrella company, Post Properties, Inc., has three affiliates: Post Atlanta, Post Management, and Post Landscape. Pretty impressive growth for a company founded on the principle of multiple breakfasts in order to hold a table!

The success of Post Properties can be traced to its philosophy, which Williams describes as a turtle's philosophy: to keep going at a steady pace, to build on the success of what has worked in the past, without succumbing to the pressure to become a rabbit, making quick moves for a quick return.

Post makes a long-term commitment to each of its developments. That means extreme care in staff and tenant

POST PROPERTIES

selection and considerable investment in landscaping and detail. Post wants to expand only into areas where the company and its developments can become a permanent force in the community, where Post can put down roots.

And put down roots it has. Much of Post's fame begins with the award-winning landscaping that is its trademark. When the company expanded into Florida, Post grew the only tulips in Orlando. They had to refrigerate them so they'd grow in the climate. Residents flocked to the leasing office to ask what exactly these exotic flowers were.

Post believes that what you see in their flowers, which can't be missed, reflects what you will find throughout their communities—attention to detail and beauty. More than one million Post flowers bloom in Atlanta alone each year, and the company has been recognized by countless national awards from landscape and architectural associations.

Service is another key to the Post success story. Repairs are completed

within twenty-four hours in 99 percent of all maintenance requests. Emergency maintenance is available evenings and weekends. Once, when an air conditioner couldn't be fixed within twenty-four hours, the residents were whisked away to a hotel, in a limo, all at Post expense.

Attention to detail is another cornerstone of the Post philosophy. Every Post apartment emphasizes comfort, peace of mind, openness, light, and storage space. Post's management firmly believes that residents want more than a place to hang their hats. Thus, recreation areas, gas grills, nature trails, car washes, clubhouses, organized activities, sports leagues, and a monthly newsletter and calendar are standard equipment, designed to turn a collection of residences into a real community.

The company's reputation for perfection and beauty has led to an active relationship with the cities Post calls home. For example, the renovation of the Marietta Square included landscaping service donated by Post. They did such a good job, in fact, that merchants around the square had to ask that the trees be cut back so their signs would show. Garden clubs, civic groups, county facilities, Boy Scout troops, YMCAs—all have benefited from the special Post touch.

The original pattern was cut for success and is still followed to this day—beautifully.

In 1973 Atlanta attorney and businessman Robert M. Fink approached Smyrna's mayor, John Porterfield, about the need for a facility to respond to the county's mental health needs. Only one free-standing psychiatric facility then existed northwest of the City of Atlanta. And it offered only fifty or so beds.

Fink envisioned a community-oriented, non-profit psychiatric hospital to serve all citizens, including adolescents and the growing number of chemically dependent patients. Making Fink's vision a reality took three years. In 1976 Ridgeview Institute opened its doors. Today, Robert Fink continues as its president and CEO.

Ridgeview is a free-standing, fully accredited, 216-bed hospital, with a wide range of outpatient services supplementing its residential programs. Its fame and recognition have spread far beyond the boundaries of Cobb County. Ridgeview is a nationally recognized leader in providing the highest possible quality of treatment for a broad spectrum of mental health and chemical dependence problems. In its fourteen years, the institute has served more than twenty-one thousand patients and their families, from all fifty states and many foreign countries.

Ridgeview's administrative independence separates it from other hospitals. One of only a handful of hospitals in the country not owned or managed by a healthcare corporation, the institute is governed by a board of directors that presently includes Fink, Porterfield, Dorothy M. Bacon, Frank B. Johnson, a past Smyrna mayor and current member of the Georgia House, Travis Duke, a former member of the state House of Representatives, and Carrollton banker H. Leroy Brock. Edward J. Osborne, executive

RIDGEVIEW INSTITUTE

vice-president of operations, and Edward A. Cone, executive vice-president of finance, are the current administrators.

The comprehensive range of programs Ridgeview offers also distinguishes it. Through its free assessment program, Ridgeview offers specialists to help people in crisis find the right treatment option when they take the crucial initial step toward recovery.

After that first step, those seeking help can choose from a wide range of services: inpatient and outpatient chemical dependence and psychiatric treatment programs specially designed for children, adolescents, and adults; programs for impaired professionals, eating disorders, sexual abuse and dissociative disorders; referral to hundreds of qualified psychiatrists, psychologists, and social workers; and extensive community education programs. Ridgeview is also committed to providing first-rate training experiences for healthcare professionals in many areas. Its large conference center is continuously used for both professional and community education programs.

Participants in all programs will benefit from Ridgeview's trademarks: a caring staff that operates as an interdisciplinary team; individual treatment planning; and a holistic approach aimed at healing the entire family, not just the individual patient.

Ridgeview is about people helping people, about shaping a mental-health care community to serve today's Cobb County.

Photo (left to right): Frank B. Johnson, John C. Porterfield, Dorothy M. Bacon, Robert M. Fink, W. Travis Duke, H. Leroy Brock.

The story of SemWare is the story of a man and his family making a dream come true.

When Sammy Mitchell graduated from college in 1980, he took his computer science degree and went to work in a large IBM mainframe shop with hundreds of other programmers. Even though he made a good living, his daily activities were not what he had envisioned as an eager student.

By 1984 he had learned enough to know that the three-piece-suit, red-tape world of corporate life was not for him. So Mitchell decided to start his own software consulting business. But even that independent plan took an unexpected turn.

One of the early applications in his consulting work required a simple text editor that would allow his client to edit and maintain files, massage reports, and browse and edit data. So

Mitchell wrote one. It turned out to be faster and more compact than any other editor he had come across.

So Mitchell began to tinker with his editor, adding features and making it completely configurable without

sacrificing ease, compactness, or speed. Everyone who tried it had one piece of advice: market it. So by mid-1985 Mitchell was seeking a software publisher for his editor.

Again, his route turned out to be different from what he had imagined. Turned down by conventional publishers intimidated by the glut of text editors already on the market, Mitchell began his own company in November 1985–SemWare. His wife, Bobbi, named his editor QEdit. They reached their first customers via electronic bulletin board systems.

At this point SemWare and QEdit were only sidelines for the Mitchells, but by early 1987 sales had been encouraging enough that Sammy Mitchell committed all his time and effort to their independent venture, working on ever more thorough and powerful versions of his original editor.

In 1989 QEdit received the Reader's Choice Award from *Data Based Advisor* for the Best Program/ Text Editor. Other publications joined in to sing QEdit's praises. And gradually the Mitchell family members and friends brought on board to make the rapidly growing company run smoothly has reached eleven–there are brothers, sisters, and even parents brought out of retirement before they could figure out what hit them.

With its current customer base in excess·of fifteen thousand, SemWare and its eleven-member team stand ready to support its existing products and customers and to develop new products to meet the challenges of the future.

And nobody has to wear a three-piece suit to work! For Sammy Mitchell and his company that's only one of many ways to measure their success.

lmost everyone agrees that man nor woman lives by bread alone. To be lived fully, life must be enriched beyond the essentials. The same is true for a community. Clear vision, a solid infrastructure, a sound economy—all are necessary, but not enough. The human spirit longs for more.

When people choose a place to live, they often fail to look beyond the essentials: are the business opportunities solid? can the government provide quality services? is adequate housing available? shopping? schools? Choosing a home is a complex decision, full of variables. Unfortunately, many remember too late to ask certain questions. They inquire about what nurtures the spirit, feeds the heart and the imagination only after they have settled in.

Where's the symphony? Is there a good museum? What sort of recreational programs are available for my kids? Can I get good Chinese food at midnight?

Of course we can survive without Chinese at midnight. Or little-league soccer. Or paintings or music or dance. We can survive. But we cannot really live.

Many people also mistakenly assume that one must choose a city, must commit to a life of major metropolitan chaos, in order to have easy and wide-ranging access to these "extras."

But that is not so. You can choose Cobb County and have it all: sound economy and unparalleled business opportunities; solid government support services; first-rate housing, schools, healthcare; a genuine vision for the future; the tranquility of suburban life in a stunning natural setting. And music and art and dance and parks and ponds and Chinese at midnight.

Choosing doesn't have to mean

eliminating. It can also mean an embarrassment of riches, looking at the newspaper and realizing that one weekend won't possibly hold it all.

Welcome to the arts, to recreation, to Cobb, where around almost every corner waits an abundance of hyacinths for the soul.

When nominations for the 1991 Academy Awards were announced, Cobb was certainly the only county in America to have two of its daughters nominated for Best Actress. Joanne Woodward spent much of her childhood in Marietta, and Julia Roberts is a native of Smyrna. Perhaps the exports currently most famous, they are more important as symbols of Cobb's rich artistic soil. Actresses and other creative things grow well here.

One reason for that fertile creative atmosphere is that Cobb's arts community knows that art isn't just for grown-ups. The Cobb Youth Museum, an educational center designed to engage elementary and middle-school classes with American history through creative participation, is typical of the approach to involvement in the arts for children. Established in 1970, the museum offers young people "the opportunity to learn about significant historical, social, and cultural events through activities emphasizing student involvement and participation," according to Anita S. Barton, its executive director.

Located adjacent to the Cheatham Hill section of Kennesaw Mountain National Battlefield Park, the museum serves more than fifteen thousand children and adults each year. School classes attend programs during the academic year, and summer programs are aimed at the general public. Role-playing involves kids directly in the learning experience. They dress in authentic costumes and participate in brief skits at each setting along the tour of the

current exhibit. Settings are carefully researched and constructed with elaborate props and rigorous attention to detail.

The museum becomes an extension of classrooms from all over the county. Curriculum advisors from the local school systems assist in the research and development of programs to ensure solid connections with formal classroom instruction. Successful exhibits from recent years include "Becoming American: The Immigrant Experience," "Transportation: From Paddles to Planes," and "American Inventors: Fathers of Industry." The museum also sponsors portable "suitcase" exhibits that bring history and science directly into the classroom. More than sixty volunteers from the Cobb County Youth Museum Guild and the Junior League of Cobb-Marietta, whose 1965 idea provided the seed for the museum, staff it and oversee its programs.

If children are interested in a purer form of theater than the museum's improvisational skits can provide, they can participate in the Cobb Children's Theatre, established in 1972. Three performances per year at the Civic Center feature children in all roles, and kids also fulfill many of the backstage functions as well. The theater also sponsors two touring groups: Vaudeville Etc. and Party Animals.

Children in Cobb can also raise their voices in the Cobb Youth Chorale, which sponsors three choirs grouped according to age and experience. The Cobb Youth Chorus of Georgia provides additional vocal opportunities. This children's chorus is dedicated to musical excellence through performance and learning. Founded in 1978 by Elizabeth Kimble, the chorus trains young singers in vocal production, music theory, sightsinging, and choral movement. The group performs throughout the year in schools and churches and at other locations for businesses and community organizations. The chorus is open to boys and girls between seven and fourteen with pleasant voices and a desire to sing.

One of Georgia's most exciting and unique arts education concepts combines the talents of two of the state's most imaginative and innovative performing companies: the TellTale Theatre and the Pandean Players. Together, they create an explosion of arts, entertainment, and education. Packaged as a traveling circus, the groups present a panorama of musical and theatrical performance spiced with samples of the visual arts and reinforced by enlightening workshops. The goal of the collaboration is to entertain, spark the imagination, encourage participation, and educate. The Arts Circus customizes programs to meet the needs of individual schools or communities, and they often incorporate into their act student art created in response to recorded versions of the music they will perform live.

They also dramatize short scenes written by students, some of which wind up as a regular feature within a TellTale sketch.

Participation is the key in all these activities. The Walker School's month-long celebration, called In Pursuit of the Arts is an extended, intensified effort to make young people active in a broad range of artistic pursuit. The program is designed to involve not only Walker students but also parents and citizens, the young and not-so-young throughout the community. All events are open to the public; they include art exhibits, musical presentations, dramatic performances, visiting authors and artists, workshops, and discovery courses.

Through active participation in the early years, one hopes to build a lifetime commitment to the arts, a commitment that will last even if one leaves the community. In this way, former Mariettan Joanne Woodward is an ideal model. She is an ongoing patron of the area's arts, having made substantial contributions to support renovation of Glover Park, the new Arts Center on Atlanta Street in Marietta, and other artistic projects.

Peggy Benson is to the arts in Cobb County what Ernest Barrett was to business and government. Raised in a musical family and a voice and drama performer herself, Benson founded the Marietta Arts Council and helped pave the way for the Cobb Civic Center. She began or has served in every arts organization in Cobb.

Singlehandedly, Benson conducted a community survey of needs in the arts. Then she teamed with Barrett to spark a bond referendum for funds to build the Civic Center. When the center opened in 1975, the first major performance, "Cherokee to Galaxies," was planned and directed by Benson. The show com-

bined and showcased the talents of all the performing groups in the county at that time.

Among the organizations that have benefited from the Benson touch are the Cobb Symphony, the Georgia Ballet, Theatre in the Square, the Children's Theatre, and the performing arts department at Kennesaw State College. Her talents also lend themselves to two community mainstays: she writes and directs the annual Singing Christmas Tree and the Last Supper madrigal performed at Marietta's First United Methodist Church. For her outstanding contributions to the arts, Benson has received the Governor's Award, and the stage in Glover Park bears her name.

The Peggy Benson-Ernest Barrett link reflects the connection between the young-turks era and Cobb's cultural boom. Longtime residents devoted to the arts found new and deep support in the wave of new citizens that washed over the county as a result of the young turks' plans. The immigrants tended to be more culturally savvy and literate than the traditional rural Cobb Countian. Between 1970 and 1980, for example, the percentage of high-school graduates among residents over age twenty-five jumped 22 percent. The number of residents with four or more years of college more than doubled in the same period. Thus, Cobb was ripe for an arts and cultural explosion.

The first Jubilee Fine Arts Festival, held over the Labor Day weekend in 1984, attracted more than fifty-five thousand. More than ten thousand school kids visited the Marietta/Cobb Fine Arts Center in the 1983-84 academic year. An explosion of galleries and other arts-related enterprises also occurred. By 1990 Cobb County offered a symphony, four community theater groups, a ballet company, a ballet guild, and four choral groups, in addition to numerous other arts activities.

To administer this burgeoning cultural growth, the county created a Department of Cultural Affairs in 1985. The department accumulates

The Cobb Arts Council, an umbrella organization of which thirty-five of the county's forty-five arts groups are members, is in part responsible for the formation of the county's Department of Cultural Affairs. The council brings together

its Romeo Hudgins Hall for sports and exhibits and the Jennie Anderson Theatre for fine arts performances. In concert with the Junior League, the council established the Arts in the Schools program, which solidifies in yet another way the tie

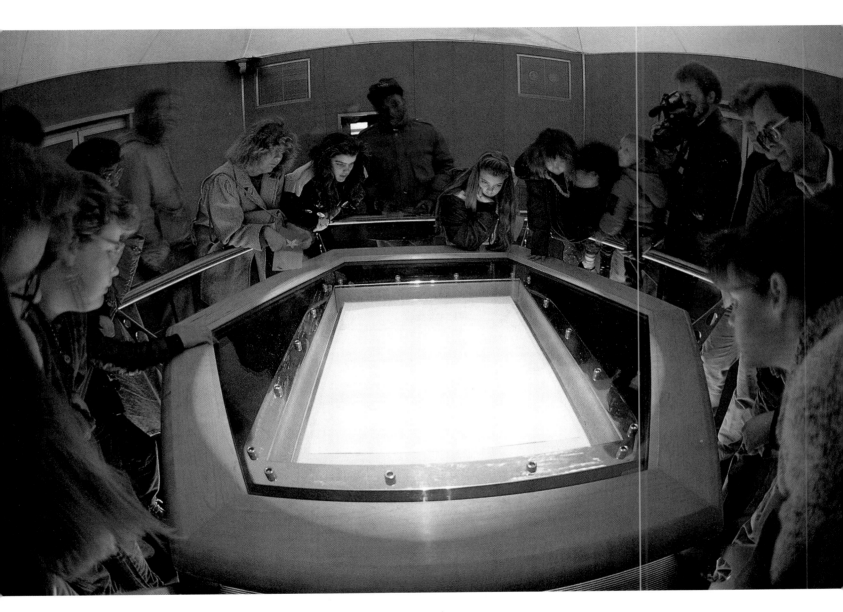

and distributes information on dozens of artists, theater groups, chorales, dance troupes, art galleries, and other enterprises in the arts. In 1988 its role expanded when it merged with the Department of Parks and Recreation. Its ten-year plan calls for, among other things, construction of a cultural arts facility in each quadrant of the county.

artists, arts organizations, and individual and corporate arts patrons for the purpose of assisting the arts community and its patrons through education, advocacy, and communications.

The first major objective undertaken by the council was to build a perfomance center in Cobb County. The result is the Civic Center, with

between children and the arts in Cobb. Brainchild of Barbara Shaw, arts coordinator for the Cobb County Schools, the annual Kaleidoscope Festival showcases the creativity of students in the Cobb County system, allowing them to exhibit or participate in every facet of the visual and performing arts. Another annual event, Salute to the Arts, awards those adults who have exhibited excellence in the various artistic disciplines and who have made outstanding contributions to the community. The proceeds from this event go to scholarships, again bringing the arts back to young people. The council's Welcome to the Arts package is designed to enhance public awareness of the wealth of cultural opportunities available in Cobb County.

Each spring since the mid-1960s the county has hosted the Cobb County Symposium, which brings to Cobb national and international experts from various disciplines to address a specific issue over a two-day period. Led by Kennesaw State College and sponsored by numerous organizations and businesses, the symposium exemplifies the hands-on community spirit that pervades attitudes toward art and culture. Among the distinguished visitors the symposium has brought to Cobb are Margaret Mead, Jonas

Salk, Richard Leakey, Norman Cousins, and William F. Buckley, Jr.

In addition to the Children's Theatre and the TellTale Theatre, Cobb offers several theatrical companies that provide a broad range of dramatic experiences. The Polk Street Players, housed at St. James Episcopal Church, numbers about twenty actors and production staff. They produce three plays each year in the Stellar Cellar at St. James. With almost two decades of experience behind them, the sixty-member Centerstage North company offers three mainstage productions and six one-acts each year. Affiliated with the Steeplehouse Arts Center, Cen-

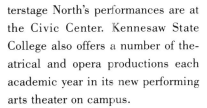

terstage North's performances are at the Civic Center. Kennesaw State College also offers a number of theatrical and opera productions each academic year in its new performing arts theater on campus.

Marietta's Theatre in the Square is the only full-time professional theater in Georgia outside Atlanta. Theatre in the Square opened in 1982. Founders Michael Horne, who serves as artistic director, and Palmer Wells, the managing director, have pushed every limit to maintain growth for the theater. In 1985 they had two hundred subscribers; in 1990, twenty-one hundred. Approximately 85 percent of the subscribers renew each year. The annual budget has ballooned from thirty-five thousand dollars to $640,000. Annual attendance has reached thirty-five thousand, about 40 percent of whom travel from outside Cobb.

Horne and Palmer have made a conscious effort to court both performers and audiences from beyond Cobb, partly out of business sense and partly because they believe diversity is essential to gaining and holding a theatrical reputation.

The theater has offered more than seventy productions; its current schedule includes five plays and one special production. One of the outfit's most talked about productions has been *Zion!*, a musical that celebrates a colorful piece of local history, the creation of the area's first

black church. An annual favorite is the holiday season show, *The 1940s Radio Hour.* When Theatre in the Square did *Trip to Bountiful,* the playwright, Horton Foote, made a point to attend.

The theater received the Governor's Award for the Arts in 1989, but it's not only Georgians who have taken note of what's going on there. New York playwrights and agents have begun to seek out the group. The Play Room, which will seat fifty to seventy-five and feature productions of experimental works, readings, and works-in-progress, opened in 1991.

Cobb offers a number of dance opportunities, including a wide variety of schools and studios to serve the amateur and the more advanced student, many of them staffed by dancers with extensive professional experience. For example, Anne Burton Avery, a former prima ballerina of the Atlanta Ballet who has also danced with the New York City Ballet under George Ballanchine, now operates the Academy of Dancing Arts in East Cobb. Home to more than eight hundred students, the school's company performs at the Kaleidoscope Festival and at Jubilee Performances at the Galleria, in addition to appearances for various civic organizations.

Another school, Dance Stop, is home to Jazz Dance Theatre South, a professional company that emphasizes theatrical preparation. At Dance Stop the philosophy is that dance can be a rewarding, fulfilling experience for students at all levels. Its complete curriculum ranges from pre-school through advanced and professional courses. The dance offerings are supplemented by drama classes.

Directed by Marcus Alford, Jazz Dance Theatre South has been featured at Charleston's world-famous Piccolo-Spoleto Festival and has toured Europe extensively. The

company is supported entirely by revenues generated by its performances, one of the few in the country to be so financed. Its repertoire includes blues and contemporary, classical, and comic jazz pieces. Jazz Dance Theatre South is gaining international recognition as one of the world's most successful jazz companies.

The Georgia Ballet, a by-product of the ballet school opened by Iris Hensley in 1957, has been entertaining patrons since 1962. Hensley, still the company's artistic director, was the first recipient of the Lillian Bennett Sullivan Award, Cobb County's highest recognition in

the arts, for inaugurating the much-imitated performing arts package for the county schools. That program and the ballet's having brought such international dance stars as Edward Villella, Medhi Bahiri, Elena Kanikova, Vanessa Howard, and Sergui Stefanschi to Cobb are good examples of how the arts community gives back to the larger community, integrating its programs and talents with the county's way of life.

In 1962 Hensley worked with sixty students; today eighteen hundred dancers at all levels study at the Georgia Ballet, and its company numbers forty, including dancers and apprentices. The annual sub-

scription series includes three programs and twelve to fifteen performances, which play to upwards of twenty thousand people each year. In addition, the group does twelve annual lecture-performances for Cobb schools. The Ballet's primary emphasis is on classical dance, but recently they have expanded their program to include more modern pieces dealing with contemporary themes. Their original works are crafted from sources as diverse as American Negro spirituals and John Denver's country ballads. Future plans include the hiring of eight to ten permanent dancers.

The Georgia Ballet's influence is not confined to Cobb County. They have performed and been well-received throughout the Southeast and in Europe. In 1977 the Ballet was instrumental in organizing the first Georgia Festival of the Arts in Sulmona, Italy. Many of its students have gone on to dance in prestigious companies nationwide.

Music rings throughout Cobb County in a variety of expressions, ranging from the Marietta Big Chicken Chorus to the Cobb Symphony Orchestra. The Big Chicken Chorus has more than one hundred members, who sing barber-shop style. After defeating many other regional choruses, the Big Chicken

singers have gone on to represent the
Dixie District in worldwide barber-
shop singing competition.

The Marietta Chorale, organized in 1965 by Jeannette Sheeler, is
a versatile group of men and women,
ages eighteen and up, from a variety
of occupations. What binds them together is a love of singing and performing for civic organizations,
nursing homes, hospitals, schools,
clubs, industry conventions, and
other audiences. The chorale presents specialty programs such as
Sing Out for America, an hour-long
extravaganza they've performed more
than two hundred times since being
chosen official ambassadors during
the 1976 bicentennial celebration.

Kerry Stevenson-Driskill founded
Mostly Chamber Music in 1986 and
continues to serve as the group's artistic director. Mostly Chamber Music presents an annual subscription
concert series that features regional
and national concert artists. The
group also conducts an annual
Young Artists competition.

In addition to their work with
the TellTale Theatre in the Arts Circus, the Pandean Players, a chamber
group founded by Barbera Secrist,
present a subscription series each
year and tour the Southeast extensively. They have participated in the
Georgia Council for the Arts Touring
Program, the South Carolina Arts
Commission Approved Artists Ros-
ter, Cobb County's Artists in the
Schools program, and the Fulton
County Arts Council's School Arts
Program. The instruments with
which the Players work their magic
are the flute, oboe, clarinet, and
bassoon, horns, and a piano.

The Cobb Symphony Orchestra
is a semi-professional group of sixty
musicians. It began in 1951 with a
ten-member volunteer instrumental
ensemble. Longtime director Betty
Shipman Bennett retired in 1990
after thirty-five years of service. She

is generally credited with the orchestra's significant growth and development.

The original ten musicians gave their first public performance in June 1952, after organizing weekly sessions for their own enjoyment. Bennett joined them in 1955, first performing in a concert at Marietta High. In 1966 the Junior League of Cobb-Marietta began to provide support and publicity, responsibilities that were assumed by the newly formed Women's Guild of the Symphony in 1972. The state of Georgia chartered the musicians in 1967, under the name Marietta Community Symphony; in 1975 it became the Cobb Community Symphony, and in 1986 assumed its current name.

The symphony has a history of playing a full range of classical, romantic, and symphonic music from the baroque to the contemporary eras. Like many other orchestras around the country, the CSO has moved from the strictly traditional to incorporate concertos, tone poems, opera excerpts, and overtures into its repertoire. Their subscription season includes four concerts at the Civic Center. They also perform an annual Christmas concert, free of charge; its program is geared toward children. Summer brings several pops concerts, performed at the Galleria and at other locations around the county.

Cobb County may surprise patrons of the visual arts. It is home to some of the most extensive collections of American art in the entire country. Attorney Fred Bentley and his wife Sarah have a collection that focuses primarily on American landscape painting of the late nineteenth and early twentieth centuries. When the Marietta/Cobb Museum of Art moved into its new headquarters in 1990, the Bentleys donated thirteen paintings from their collection to enhance the museum's holdings.

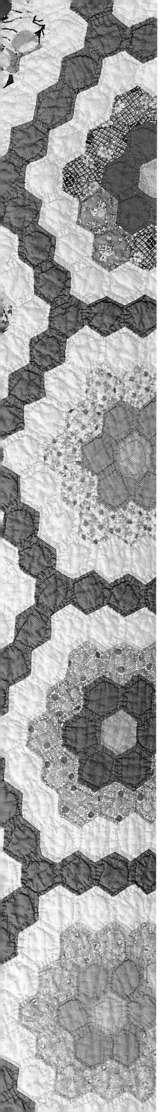

Louise and Alan Sellars have collected some of the best work by nineteenth- and twentieth-century women artists. They began this focused collection in 1984 and now have five hundred paintings from three hundred artists, primarily women from the Northeast and Midwest. The University of Michigan Slide Distribution Project has arranged for the Sellars's collection to be copied and distributed to universities across the country. Theirs is the first private collection the project has selected for its files.

Dr. and Mrs. Noah Meadows have an impressive collection of eighteenth- and nineteenth-century American art that includes landscapes and impressionistic pieces. Dr. Meadows's favorites are by the Wyeths while his wife is partial to the work of Lamar Dodd. The Meadowses have shared their collection and their time and energies with the art museum, Kennesaw State College, and other institutions. Dr. Meadows is the recipient of the Governor's Award for the Arts and of the Liberty Bell Award.

The Marietta/Cobb Museum of Art has its origins in the Marietta Fine Arts Club, begun in 1973 by a group of artists interested in fostering the community's cultural growth. In 1983 the group found a home in the former Clarke Library building on Church Street and became the Marietta/Cobb Fine Arts Center. The new facility allowed for the display of exhibits and for classes to be taught. Among the museum's educational programs are courses in pottery, drawing, watercolors, photography, portraiture, techniques and media, and creative interpretation and movement. Children and adults can study at the museum, and kids can also enjoy Art Camp, a series of three two-week sessions during the summer, and an annual Children's Art Festival.

Success breeds growth, and in 1990 the fine arts center became the Marietta/Cobb Museum of Art and moved into its new headquarters in the former central library building on Atlanta Street, just off the square in Marietta. The new facility offers three separate galleries for the museum's growing collection donated by local collectors. Funded by private and corporate donations, the Cobb County Arts Commission, the Georgia Council for the Arts, and the city of Marietta, the museum has plans for subsequent renovation of its building to create workshop and meeting space, offices, an art library, and a permanent hands-on exhibit for children.

©Jane Gardner Preston

Known throughout the Southeast and even the country as a haven for antiques and other collectibles, Cobb County offers two specialized museums for the avid doll collector or fan. Both are located in the town of Kennesaw. The Doll Gallery has three to five thousand dolls of all kinds. The Mauldin Doll Museum's collection offers another twenty-five hundred of the beloved toys.

Sometimes the worlds of business and art overlap, as in the case of the Lillie Glass Blowers in Smyrna. Lillie is the only group in the country doing both scientific and decorative work. Their artisans transform rods of crystal into things of beauty and usefulness, including laboratory instruments, free-form sculptures, achievement awards, Christmas ornaments, and Galileo thermoscopes. They have even created a life-sized glass baby for a television commercial.

Smyrna is also home to the Cobb Photographic Society, one of the area's largest camera clubs, with more than one hundred continuous members. The society's goal is to provide a meeting place where photographers of all ability levels can exchange ideas about all aspects of photography. They present lectures or other programs at bimonthly meetings, organize model shoots, including field trips for outdoor experience, and sponsor intra-club competitions with outside judges, who offer unbiased critiques. The society also sponsors the annual Cobb Photo Salon, a photography contest open to all photographers. In a typical year, as many as seven hundred images will be entered.

Cobb offers two multi-purpose arts centers to its citizens. One is the Mable House in Mableton. In addition to housing the various administrative groups that its does, including the South Cobb Arts Alliance, the Mable House is home to an Arts Center that is open to the public Tuesday through Saturday each week. Also available are art classes for children and adults and summer classes for kids. The Mable House sponsors an ongoing series of exhibits, an annual art auction, a Candlelite Concert Series, and the Literary Round Table, a writers' group.

History comes to life at the an-nual "Gone with the Wind" Party at the Mable House, and the "Trash to Treasures" exhibit, sponsored by the Cobb Clean Commission, combines art with environmental concerns in a nod to the needs of the future. For this exhibit, students create works of art from discarded objects. Two arts-and-crafts extravaganzas take place at the Mable House each year: in April the Sweetwater Fever Fine Arts & Crafts Festival and in September the Sweetwater Valley Fine Arts &

Crafts Festival.

Plans for the future at the Mable House include construction of the Mable Center for Community and Cultural Affairs, which will feature a $650,000 twelve-hundred-seat amphitheatre and the re-creation of a historical village.

East Cobb is home to the Steeplehouse Arts Center, which offers an extensive curriculum of art classes for children and adults. The philosophy at Steeplehouse is pro-

cess-oriented, not project-oriented, and the focus is on art as a teaching tool. "Artsy," the center's pink-and-purple dragon visits thirty to fifty schools each year to introduce a puppet-making project. The center also sponsors theater and cabaret performance groups for teens.

The Steeplehouse Art Gallery showcases the work of Cobb artists and, in addition to its art classes, the center conducts summer camps and courses in the literary and per-

forming arts. Home to Centerstage North, Steeplechase has a small stage for dramatic presentations.

The center heads for its new home in the East Cobb Community Arts Center in fall 1991. The county has allocated $1.3 million dollars for a 13,500-square-foot facility, with six studios, a gallery, a 250-seat theater, a conference room, and offices.

Much about the arts scene in Cobb is exciting. Already in place are first-rate organizations in almost

every area of artistic endeavor. Community and government support is strong. Growth has been and continues to be impressive and carefully planned. But if one had to characterize the arts in only one word, that word might be participatory. Many communities seem to rope the arts off, make them something out there, to look at and admire and wonder about, but not to do. Not so in Cobb. Here, the arts are truly for the people. All they must do is do.

he same is certainly true of sports and other recreational activities. Even if someone wants only to play, nothing else, just play, Cobb could keep that person busy for quite a while.

Whether one participates or watches, Cobb teems with leisure opportunities. Its high-school sporting events are among the best-attended in the metro area. In 1983 East Marietta won the Little League World Series. The county alone operates thirty-five parks and recreation centers, covering twenty-six hundred acres devoted to picnic areas, pavilions, jogging trails, multi-purpose courts, fitness trails, and playgrounds. And this doesn't even take into account the facilities available in the numerous community parks. The Cobb Aquatics Center is a year-round facility with two heated indoor pools, a diving well, and a fitness center, so it's possible to exercise without ever going outside, if that's what suits the fancy.

The most visited park in the county is probably the Kennesaw Mountain National Battlefield Park, which hosts 2.5 million visitors each year, making it one of the top ten of the country's three hundred national parks. Its twenty-nine hundred acres

include eleven miles of original earthworks left from the famous battle fought there. A Visitors' Center museum features exhibits that capture the daily life of a Civil War soldier. The park has a number of interesting hiking trails; the longest is sixteen miles round-trip, and the shortest is a one-mile walk to the top of Big Kennesaw Mountain.

Another piece of history has been preserved just outside the boundaries of the park. Kolb's Farm is the restored home of Peter Valentine Kolb. On June 22, 1864, Union General Joseph Hooker took the house as his headquarters following a battle north of Powder Springs. Visitors can see what the farm would have looked like when Hooker and his troops moved in.

A September tradition in Cobb is the North Georgia State Fair, which has showcased the region's growth and development from a rural, agricultural area to one of the nation's fastest-growing locations. Founded in the late 1800s by the Cobb County Fair Association, the fair created a new brand of excitement for farmers and their families, who were at that time growing mostly cotton and raising livestock.

After being re-chartered and changing locations several times, the fair settled into its current location on Callaway Road in 1966. Its charter was amended and its name changed to the North Georgia State Fair in 1967. A 1955 premium catalog stated the goals of the fair association: "to bring together for display the best livestock, agricultural and home products made and grown in the county; to display educational exhibits and conduct demonstrations . . .; and to provide a place where all can go for recreation and entertainment." Although clearly a reflection of the county's rural roots, as early as 1960 the fair was also looking forward to the future. In that pre-liberation era, it changed the name of its handwork exhibits from "Women's Work" to "Handwork Women's and Men's."

If the fair reminds us of our past, Worldfest is a celebration of

the future and the increasingly global sense of our world. Conceived in 1983, the program was so well-received that it generated a separate nonprofit organization, One World Foundation, Inc. Worldfest is an international festival of art and culture. In 1989 more than sixty thousand people enjoyed 120 performing artists from twenty different countries, international food, and a marketplace bazaar. The goal of Worldfest is to foster relationships in the international community and to generate interest in a more accurate understanding of other cultures.

In this rapidly growing area, the fastest-growing recreational activity is softball. The hub of the action is the Al Bishop Softball Complex in Marietta, named for a former Marietta Parks and Recreation director. Bishop served for thirty-six years as commissioner of the Amateur Softball Association in Georgia.

Seventeen thousand men and women on eight hundred teams play

softball in Cobb. The leagues include open, church, and industrial competition, playing slow-pitch, fast-pitch, modified fast-pitch, and co-ed ball.

Another rapidly growing sport is soccer. Two new complexes have been recently built; between them they have fifteen fields. Cobb also loves tennis. The county alone provides ninety-two courts. There are numerous tournaments and a year-round Cobb Tennis League. Participation in the American Lawn Tennis Association, its teams and tournaments, is higher in the Atlanta area than anywhere else in the country. Cobb County alone fields five hundred ALTA teams.

Larry Bell Park, named for the president of the Bell Aircraft Corporation, is a forty-five-acre complex adjacent to the Civic Center. In addition to the Cobb Aquatics Center, the park is home to the Cobb Gymnastics Center, one of the metro area's largest instructional programs. The center also sponsors competitions and is home to the Cobb Challenger Gymnastic Team.

The Cobb County Parks and Recreation Department was established in 1966; in 1989 it merged with the Department of Cultural Affairs to become the Department of Parks, Recreation, and Cultural Affairs. More than 150 people staff the department, and in 1989 5.2 million people participated in its programs or used its facilities. One purpose of the 1989 reorganization was to place more emphasis on recreation programming and activities and less on revenue-producing programs and facilities. In other words, the goal was to shift the focus from making money to serving people.

The Cobb parks and recreation system is one of the Southeast's largest. A seven-member Recreation Commission acts as an advisory board to determine needs and make recommendations. Programs include: softball, tennis, track and field, swimming, gymnastics, football, volleyball, basketball, and soccer. Facilities include show rings, a BMX race track, batting cages, and horseshoe courts. The travel division plans trips for citizen groups to such diverse locales as Callaway Gardens, Colorado Springs, New York City, and Hawaii. A special programs unit provides activities for special populations, among them the mentally and physically handicapped.

In addition to the county facilities, each of the six incorporated communities has its own recreation and parks program. The one in Marietta is typical, offering group meet-

ings and classes in everything from golf to porcelain painting. It also sponsors summer day camps for children ages four to twelve and "Safety Town," a two-week program for four- and five-year-olds that promotes safety issues by using a mock town set-up. Activities for senior citizens include a photography group, a walking club, and the Senior Olympics.

Cobb is home to at least ten golf courses, and each spring the PGA Tour comes to the county for the BellSouth Atlanta Classic. The tournament represents BellSouth's first sponsorship of a major national sporting event. Held at the Atlanta Country Club in East Cobb, the Atlanta Classic has donated nearly two million dollars to charity since 1982. More than one million dollars has gone to its principal charity, Henrietta Egleston Hospital for Children, which in 1988 received the PGA Tour's first "Charity of the Year"

award. Nineteen eighty-nine's record-breaking gift of $452,000 represents an almost 60 percent increase from the previous year.

More than 100,000 people attend the Classic, and that doesn't include the millions more who watch it on television. In 1967 Bob Charles won the tournament and twenty-two thousand dollars; Scott Simpson, the 1989 winner, took home $162,000, demonstrating that growth in Cobb is contagious in many ways. Past winners of the Classic include Jack Nicklaus, Hale Irwin, Tom Watson, and Tom Kite. The record low score for four rounds is 265, shared by Andy Bean (1979) and Dave Barr (1987). But perhaps nothing has pleased Classic galleries more than the 1980 and 1988 wins by Larry Nelson, a Cobb County native himself.

The Chattahoochee River has been crucial to Cobb County in many ways, recreation included. In 1978 a Congressional act created a sixty-eight-thousand-acre National Recreation Area along forty-eight miles of the river, much of it in Cobb County, to preserve and protect its

scenic, historic, and recreational aspects. The National Park Service, which administers the recreation area, offers guided nature walks on which guides point out historical highlights, including remnants of early Indian life, and wildlife.

The river is regularly stocked with brook, rainbow, and brown trout and is classified as a Georgia Designated Trout Stream. The Cochran Fitness Trail is a three-mile activity path open to pedestrians, wheelchairs, and bicycles. Twenty-two exercise stations are located along the trail, which offers a number of breathtaking river views. The Sope Creek section features trails that go past the ruins of two paper mills dating back to Civil War days.

But the most popular river activity is rafting down its water. Four put-in points are available: Jones Bridge, Morgan Falls, Johnson Ferry, and Powers Island. The Chattahoochee Outdoor Center has rental and put-in facilities at Johnson Ferry and Powers Island and take-out facilities at Powers Island and Paces Mill. They can provide four-, six-, and eight-man rafts, canoes, kayaks, lifejackets, paddles, and coolers. A shuttle service connects the three sites, with food, beverages, and sundries available at all three. The center can also provide instructional clinics and catered picnics.

Another nature-oriented park within Cobb is the Wildwood Nature Park in Marietta. Its twenty-eight-acre site includes a one-third-mile, self-guided Sensory Trail for the Blind.

The largest man-made lake in the county is Lake Allatoona. There, and at nearby Lake Acworth, fishermen will find both pier and boat fishing available, with recreation and picnic areas nearby. Lake Allatoona is a favorite of swimmers, windsurfers, sailors, and motorboaters. Tents and RVs dot its campgrounds, and

picnickers keep the grills going. A dozen camping areas and public recreation sites are located on the lake. Park attendants for the Allatoona Wildlife Management Area maintain

boat-launching ramps, fishing jetties, hiking trails, grills, beaches, and group shelters, which can be reserved.

Another favorite summer spot is Sun Valley Beach in Powder Springs. A huge pool with slides and other features is surrounded by a sandy beach. Tennis, softball, volleyball, and basketball can be enjoyed only steps away from the beach. The staff can provide party planning and catering.

Cobb residents and tourists alike flock to the county's three theme parks: White Water, American Adventures, and Six Flags over Georgia. White Water is the largest and most visited waterpark in the South, with thirty-five acres of water attractions and more than 700,000 visitors per year. Opened in 1983, the waterpark offers more than two dozen specialty water rides and activities. Among the favorites are the Atlanta Ocean, with four-foot waves for body-surfing; Roaring Rapids; Caribbean Plunge; Black River

Falls; Little Squirts Island; and the Bermuda Triangle. More than two thousand lounge chairs, rafts, and lifejackets are provided. Red Cross-certified lifeguards oversee the fun, and visitors can use lockers and showers and enjoy three restaurants and gift shops.

American Adventures opened in 1990 on ten acres just outside the White Water complex. The indoor theme park also features outdoor adventures, such as miniature golf, a racetrack, and bumper cars; family rides; a children's play area; a penny arcade; and a family-style restaurant. The Victorian-inspired complex is reminiscent of an old-fashioned town square, complete with an antique carousel and calliope music. The park is open year-round and offers party facilities.

The granddaddy of Cobb's theme parks is Six Flags over Georgia, which packs an amazing array of fun into its 331 acres. The Southern Star Amphitheatre hosts top performers from rock, country, and contemporary Christian music. October brings a Halloween Spectacular, and from Thanksgiving through December, there's Holiday in the Park, a winter festival complete with carollers, ice skating, and a ton of snow and two miles of garlands. And lights: 910,000 tiny bulbs and seven thousand large red and green bulbs that transform the Great Gasp ride into a giant Christmas tree.

In fact, Six Flags is a pretty well-lighted place year-round. Its Shows Department uses 12,578 light bulbs in an average season, with 21,208 additional bulbs being used to light rides, buildings, street lamps, walkways, and parking lots. It's also a beautifully landscaped operation, using fifteen hundred hanging baskets each year and orchestrating three annual rounds of planting, with a total of 100,000

flowers and plants.

But rides have made Six Flags famous. Among the favorites is the Georgia Cyclone, patterned after the legendary Coney Island Cyclone. Its construction required 500,000 board-feet of lumber, five thousand gallons of paint, and 925 concrete piers. The Great American Scream Machine is another crowd-pleaser. It consumed 750,000 board-feet of lumber, enough for three two-story wooden houses; seventeen tons of bolts and four tons of nails; and thirty-six hundred gallons of paint. Thunder River, a water ride, requires two million gallons of water to keep it going. Each minute 334,000 gallons are pumped to the ride.

No matter which of the park's hundreds of activities visitors choose, they can rest assured that their experience will be safe and pleasant. The park's top priority is to provide safe family fun for the millions who come there each year.

While cultural and recreational programs serve the mind and body, Cobb's churches tend the spirit. They also involve themselves in almost every social program and charitable concern in the community. From the earliest days, when Smyrna grew from a religious campground, to today's complex urban environment, churches have been a center for and a focal point of life in Cobb.

The camp-meeting origins of religious life in the county live on in the annual Marietta Camp Meeting. This East Cobb revival dates back to 1837, making it one of the county's oldest traditions. Although organized by the United Methodist Church, the camp meeting is interdenominational. For ten days each August worshippers come to a twenty-two-acre site near the intersection of Roswell and Sewell Mill roads in Marietta. There they find century-old cabins and a tin-roofed worship tent, in which they sing hymns, listen to sermons, and participate in prayer meetings to revitalize all who come and to renew their commitment of faith. The camp meeting is the scene of many reunions among families and longtime friends. Some of the cabins have sawdust floors, a reminder of the old days when campers brought livestock that occupied the lower level while the people stayed upstairs.

More than three hundred churches in the county represent twenty-three denominations, providing a broad range of worship experiences and philosophies for citizens. Among the most interesting historically is Zion Baptist Church on Lemon Street in Marietta. Zion was added to the National Register of Historic Places in 1990 and has been the subject of a much-acclaimed musical at Theatre in the Square.

The first black Baptist church in Marietta, Zion was founded in 1866 in a building on the corner of Lemon and Haynes streets. In 1978 the church moved into a new building on Lemon Street. Prior to 1866, Marietta's black Baptists worshipped with their white masters at First Baptist Church, where the first black member was received and enrolled on January 9, 1836. In May 1856 the members of First Baptist voted to allow blacks to secure a separate place of worship while remaining members of First Baptist. They also agreed that the blacks could elect two deacons. On April 8, 1866, Zion Baptist Church was formally organized, with the Reverend Ephraim B.

Rucker as pastor.

The oldest church in Cobb is Mt. Bethel Methodist Church, which celebrated its 150th anniversary in 1990. The church, which began in 1840 with thirteen charter members, was originally called Bethel Methodist-Episcopal Church and was located on Lower Roswell Road about a half-mile east of Johnson Ferry Road. In the late 1870s two acres of land at the intersection of Lower Roswell and Johnson Ferry were donated for a new building. Until 1950, when classrooms were added, the church remained a one-room building. Today Mt. Bethel is home to three thousand members.

The increasing diversity in Cobb's population is reflected in the diversity of its churches. For example, in August 1989 Holy Transfiguration Greek Orthodox Church formed to serve the needs of 160 families. The church has met in the Sprayberry Crossing Shopping Center as it works toward construction of

a sanctuary.

One of the most famous and darkest chapters in Cobb's history involves the 1915 lynching of Jewish businessman Leo Frank, a story that has been the subject of several books and a television movie starring Jack Lemmon. From that dark past Cobb has emerged in the 1980s as home to several thriving synagogues and more Jewish children than any county in metro Atlanta.

In the same month that Holy Transfiguration began meeting in the shopping center, the Jewish Community Center opened its doors. The center is home to Temple Kol Emeth until its 220-family membership can construct a synagogue. The center, part of a nonprofit agency that serves metropolitan Atlanta, provides social, recreational, cultural, and educational programs. It is commited to programs and services that will expand and enhance members' Jewish identification.

Located in Shirley Blumenthal Park in Marietta, the center has a junior Olympic pool and a kiddie pool, a bathhouse, a preschool, a mothers' morning-out program, meeting rooms, playing fields, six acres of wooded park, and a two-acre lake. Emblematic of Cobb's progress as a community that respects and honors diversity, the center also reflects the way that life in Cobb is a seamless fabric of pleasure and commitment and rich experience.

Generations of school children have grown up with the legend involving the 1898 marble statue of Mary Meinert in the St. James Episcopal Cemetery across the street from Marietta High. The story says that the statue, which portrays Mary holding two infants in her arms, weeps at midnight on every Friday the 13th. Thus, the schoolyard chant, passed down from one generation to the next: "Mary, Mary, why did your babies die?"

CAMILLE SESSIONS HEGG

When I was a child, I visited my grandmother in Marietta. We would walk to the square from her home on Church Street to shop. She never needed to drive. One summer, we walked to the square to buy me a pair of shoes at Coggins. I can still do that, but I also have access to the malls and shopping centers. When I have my car repaired, I know the people who work on it. But I can also follow my grandmother's example and not drive at all because of today's efficient public transportation.

The "four-lane" was a very busy road for my grandmother, but today's Cobb Parkway would be beyond her imagination. I remember her proudly showing me the Cobb County Times and telling me that Marietta had grown to eight thousand people.

When I moved here, the place had a special feeling. I sensed that I could touch some roots. We first lived in an apartment on Terrell Mill Road, surrounded by woods. Moving into Marietta offered a smaller school system for my child and closer proximity to my work. I now live in the historic district off the square, just like my grandmother.

As something of a city person, I find the cultural atmosphere here more than satisfying. I've watched the symphony grow and its audiences increase. I've seen the old library become the art museum and the new library open. Stepping Stones, a sculpture by a local artist, was donated to the library by citizens, completing a circle of art appreciation.

Cobb's reverence for the past is matched by a commitment to the future. I especially appreciate recycling and other programs to protect the environment.

Camille Sessions Hegg is Associate Rector of St. James Episcopal Church.

157

T hat custom aside, little about the past haunts Cobb County. The past is revered and preserved, but it is the past. The lifestyle enjoyed here is very much a matter of the present and even the future. And life is enjoyed.

Cobb County's residents have the highest average household income in metropolitan Atlanta and the highest annual per capita income, at more than forty-two thousand dollars. More than 32 percent of households in 1986 had a disposable personal income in excess of fifty thousand dollars. In 1988 the average home price was $125,000; for a three-bedroom home, $142,000. The Homestead Exemption for homeowners is also the highest in the metro area.

Certainly, small-town activities proceed almost as if time has stood still, but every economic indicator shouts that it hasn't. The richness of the Cobb lifestyle, both in economic and experiential terms, would be almost unimaginable to the pre-boom citizens who lived here prior to World War II and have not survived to see Cobb in the nineties. And if it would be unimaginable to them, what would those original settlers think? The ones who came with visions of gold and stayed to become hard-scrabble farmers—perhaps they would think that there was, in fact, gold of a different sort, the gold of opportunity.

How does Cobb spend that disposable income? Well, it shops, in more than one hundred shopping centers and several malls. The retail scene is a virtual melting pot of large chains, specialty shops, and discount centers. The Cobb Center, now called Four Seasons, was the county's first enclosed mall when it opened in 1962. Cumberland Mall followed in 1973, with its four anchor stores and almost 150 specialty shops. The Galleria opened across

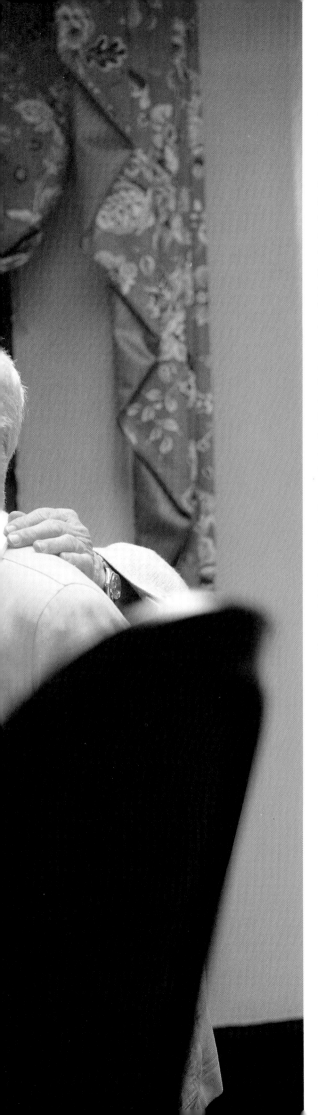

U.S. 41 from Cumberland in 1982, and the Platinum Triangle began to emerge as the business and retail hotspot of the county.

Town Center at Cobb, the newest of the malls, opened in 1986. It features four anchor stores and more than 175 specialty shops. Town Center is also typical of the way that all the malls have begun to enter into many facets of community life beyond the traditional retailer's role. Town Center sponsors a mall-walking exercise program supervised by Kennestone Hospital. A similar program, supervised by Cobb Hospital and Medical Center, is housed at Four Seasons. Town Center also sponsors a Community Day program as a fundraiser for nonprofit organizations; Cumberland hosts an annual College Fair in the fall to provide information to prospective college students and their parents. All the malls have been active in the success of the Cobb Community Transit system and its programs, in the Partners in Education program, and in recycling and other community ecological programs.

If shoppers long for a more old-fashioned shopping experience than the malls provide, Vinings and the Marietta Square areas can oblige them. Shopping in East Cobb is concentrated along Johnson Ferry Road, with four major complexes: Merchants Walk, Providence Square, Fountains at Old Town, and Parkaire Landing, which has its own ice-skating rink.

In 1941 Harry Strother moved his Ford dealership from downtown Marietta to the "four-lane," as natives referred to U.S. 41. At the time the four-lane was bordered mostly by vacant land. Today more than twenty car dealerships have followed Strother's lead. They sell almost every make and model, domestic and foreign, a buyer could desire.

You can get Chinese food at midnight, but what else does Cobb offer in the way of cuisine? Almost everything.

Two famous restaurants hearken back to the county's origins in their setting and their presentation. Aunt Fanny's Cabin has been providing a taste of the Old South to its customers since 1941. Its building, formerly slave quarters, dates back to 1840, and the restaurant is named for Aunt Fanny Williams, who was born and lived on the property. The traditional menu features fried chicken, turnip greens, cornbread, and squash casserole. Aunt Fanny's Singers entertain diners with traditional hymns and blues numbers.

Equally historic is The Planters, located in an 1848 Greek Revival mansion surrounded by thirteen landscaped acres. Known as the Glover-McLeod-Garrison House, the home is listed in the National Register of Historic Places. The Planters comes equipped with its own ghost, believed to be the grandmother or great-grandmother of a former resident family. She wears a grandmotherly sweet cologne, first smelled in the wine cellar. Employees report that the ghost has rearranged furniture, broken glassware, and extinguished candles that then mysteriously reignite. The menu does include some dishes that honor the establishment's southern roots,

but a typical evening is more in keeping with a fine continental dining experience.

Another restaurant with historic atmosphere is Shillings on the Square. Housed in the 1935 building that was once home to Shillings Hardware, the downstairs pub has a 120-year-old bar and lovely stained glass. The pub serves from a casual menu while upstairs diners enjoy candlelight elegance and piano music as they sample first-rate American and continental cuisine.

Another atmosphere altogether reigns at Carey's Place, the archetypal "redneck honkytonk," to use its manager's description. The manager describes its jukebox as "very off-color"; radio station Y-106 voted it the best country jukebox in Atlanta. But visitors to Carey's will usually find the restaurant inhabited by a broader spectrum of Cobb's and metro Atlanta's population than these details might suggest. The reason? The best hamburgers in Atlanta, according to almost every source that rates such things.

The Galleria is home to several premier dining establishments. In the Stouffer Waverly Hotel Sunday brunch is a sight to behold. Some consider it the brunch to end all brunches, with more than 150 foods to choose from.

Outside the hotel, but still within the Galleria, is Winfield's, which serves from an American-continental menu in a setting that has won awards for its design. Patterned after a 1920s ballroom, the restaurant features twenty-foot ceilings, mosaic-tiled pillars and floor, and palm trees scattered throughout. The piano lounge, with its marble-topped bar, is also an award-winner, as are Winfield's famous desserts.

Kiefer's, a neighborhood gathering place for West Mariettans, features fresh seafood on its menu. *Inside Cobb* magazine voted it the

©Jane Gardner Preston

county's best casual restaurant.

And, if ethnic food is your desire, you can enjoy Indian cuisine at Haveli, surrounded by sitar music and the aroma of authentic spices. Or there's Italian at Montecalvo's or Scalini's. *Atlanta Magazine* called Montecalvo's lasagna the city's best while Scalini's is reportedly the Italian restaurant of choice for other restaurant owners. Scalini's is a visual as well as a dining feast, decorated to recall the authentic thing in Italy and alive with oversized stuffed animals and food transformed into *objets d'art*.

Although not open till midnight, the House of Chan has frequently been named the best Chinese restaurant in metro Atlanta. The owners import hard-to-find Chinese herbs and spices, Chinese ham and table wines, and dried, fragrant onions. The house specialty is steamed whole snapper or grouper with ginger and scallions, black bean sauce, and fresh pepper. Off the square in Marietta, Greek food is available at Jimmy's on the Square, a favorite gathering spot for the county's politicians and government officials.

And these are only the surface of the hundreds of dining options available all over Cobb. There's so much good food that the number of health clubs and other exercise opportunities is essential, not a frill. Without them Cobb would never be able to keep its collective weight under control. The temptations are too many and too strong.

If there's any energy left after a special dinner out, Cobb has nightlife too. In addition to the many, many possibilities offered by the arts community, from the symphony to Theatre in the Square to the Georgia

Ballet or Jazz Dance Theatre South, Studebaker's offers dancing to an oldies soundtrack. A Comic Cafe allows patrons to sit and listen to the top stand-up comics on national tour. Perhaps the largest nightspot in Cobb is Miss Kitty's Saloon and Dance Hall. On an average weekend two to three thousand customers come to enjoy top country entertainment acts and to dance on one of the largest dance floors in the state. On Mondays and Tuesdays beginners can take free lessons in the Texas Two-Step, the Cotton-Eyed Joe, and other staples of country-and-western dance.

And if you're too full from your dinner for anything active at all, try a carriage ride around Marietta's square and through the historic district. This perfect, quiet ending to a lively modern night out takes us right back to the beginnings and reminds us that change and tradition working hand-in-hand is the best of all possible worlds.

What does it feel like to live in Cobb County, Georgia? In its 1989-90 report to its citizens, the Board of Commissioners said that Cobb blends "the best of urban living with a reverence for a quiet, more peaceful pace. . . . that successful mix of town and country lifestyle—good neighborhoods and business locations amid continuous and well-managed growth."

That is a fair and accurate assessment. But commission reports alone can never capture the vitality, the energy, the very pulse of this place. The words and pictures of this book are the first step, we hope, in making this place in this time real, tangible for newcomers and lifetime residents and visitors. Welcome to the heart of Cobb, a community at the heart of change. Feel its pulse. Study its soul. Allow yourself to enter into the powerful current of its amazing story. And enjoy.

ACKNOWLEDGMENTS

Each of the following corporate profile companies made a valuable contribution to this project. Longstreet Press gratefully acknowledges their participation.

The Art of Y.S. Piero Designs & Associates
Barnett Bank of Atlanta
BellSouth Atlanta Classic
Brawner Psychiatric Institute
Childress-Klein Properties/Atlanta Galleria
City of Marietta/Marietta Power
Cobb County Community Improvement District
Cobb Electric Membership Corporation
Cobb Hospital & Medical Center
Confederation Life
Cousins Properties/Wildwood Office Park
Egleston Children's Hospital
The Georgian Club/Indian Hills Country Club
Healthdyne, Incorporated
Kennestone Regional Health Care System
Lockheed Aeronautical Systems Company
Murata-Erie North America
Post Properties
Ridgeview Institute
SemWare Software Products

This book was published in cooperation with the Cobb Chamber of Commerce and would not have been possible without the support of its members. Longstreet Press is especially grateful to the following individuals for their commitment and for their continued assistance.

Gay Watson
Phil Sanders
Jane Gardner Preston
Dave Kaplan

We would also like to thank the following individuals who contributed in a variety of ways to the quality of **Cobb County: At the Heart of Change.**

Ken Bartlett, The Georgia Ballet
Robert Crowe, Hardy Studio
Anne Marie Crowell, Dobbins Air Force Base
Marcel David, Cobb Historical Society
Jeff Findlay, KSA Associates, Inc.
Lee Garner, Marietta Cobb Museum of Art
Anna Garretson, Cobb Symphony Orchestra
Dave Garrison, Kennesaw State College
Ed Hoback, Marietta Power
Zada Jackson, Mable House
Theresa Jenkins, Marietta Welcome Center
Dick Martin, Lockheed Aeronautical Systems Company
Beth O'Brien, Beaux Arts Ball
Addie Schneider, Temple Kol Emeth
Elaine Separk, Mount Bethel Methodist Church
Lisa Shirley, Vinings Overlook
Rachel Schrauner, Cobb Community Transit System
Ken Smalley, KSA Associates, Inc.
Dorothy Summerour, Mount Bethel Methodist Church
Palmer Wells, Theatre in the Square
Glenda Willoughby, Cobb Arts Council

The following publications were especially helpful in providing information for the text.

Roth, Darlene R. *Architecture, Archaelology and Landscapes.* Cobb County: Cobb County Historic Preservation Commission, 1988.

Atlanta Business Chronicle
Atlanta Journal & Constitution, Cobb Annual Report
Marietta Daily Journal, Cobb Annual Report

PHOTOGRAPHY CAPTIONS

Front end	Cotton farmers on Marietta Square (circa 1910)
ii	Robert Goodman, Oakton, Marietta
v	Worldfest 1990
vi	Mt. Bethel Methodist Church, Marietta
viii	Rafters on the Chattahoochee River
2, 3	Sandy Marino, Austell
4, 5	Atlanta's skyline from Vinings
6, 7	Aerial view of the Galleria Complex
8A	Watermelons, Kennesaw
8B	Tomatoes, Powder Springs
9	Man with grandson, Kennesaw
10, 11	Railroad crossing, Marietta
12, 13	Demolition team worker, Austell
14	Lost Mountain Store, between Marietta and Dallas
15	Will, Brenda & Chris Sumpter fishing on a neighborhood pond, Kennesaw
16, 17	Dobbins Air Force Base, home to the Naval Air Station and the Georgia Air National Guard, Marietta
18	Construction workers, Marietta
19	Helen VanderHorst
20, 21	Marietta resident in front of her home
22	Kennesaw House, Marietta
23	Marietta National Cemetery
24	Marietta Depot
25A	Howell House, Marietta
25B	Marlow House, Marietta
26A	Worldfest 1990
26B	Worldfest 1990
26C	Worldfest 1990
27	Glover Park, Marietta
28, 29	The Big Chicken, Marietta
30	Acworth residents
31	Jet-skiers on Lake Allatoona, Acworth
32	Children in field, Austell
33A	Construction, Cobb County subdivision
33B	*The General,* Big Shanty Museum, Kennesaw
34, 35	Kennesaw Mountain National Battlefield Park
36, 37	Proprietor Dent Myers, Wildman's, Kennesaw
38, 39	Kennesaw family
40A	Sun Valley Beach, Powder Springs
40B	McEachern High School campus, Powder Springs
41	Railroad tracks, Powder Springs
42	Smyrna residence
43A	Little girl in field, Smyrna
43B	Concord Covered Bridge, Smyrna
44, 45	Marietta subdivision
45	Trey Moores
46, 47	East Cobb subdivision
48, 49	Beaux Arts Ball, The Galleria, Smyrna
50	Aerial view of downtown Vinings
51	Atlanta's skyline from Vinings
52, 53	Mable House exhibit, Mableton
53	Jack Boone
54, 55	Baby, Kennesaw
56	Hui Sun and Song Tae Pak, owners of The Oyster King, Kennesaw
57	Georgia General Assembly
58, 59	Marietta firefighter
60	The Galleria, Smyrna
61	Highway US 41
62	CCT bus on route, Marietta Square
63A	Austell road
63B	Austell road
64	Student doing research in library
65	Volunteers, Seniors' Day, North Georgia Fair
66	Garden, Oakton, Marietta
67	Oakton, Marietta
68, 69	Patient undergoing eye examination
70	Westside Elementary School, Marietta
71	Give Our Schools A Hand '89 Program, Donna Milton, Marietta City Schools, Wes McCoy, Cobb County Schools, Marietta Square
73A	Marietta High homecoming parade 1990
73B	Japanese Saturday School
73C	Computer lab in Cobb County school

74, 75	Wheeler High homecoming 1990
75	College student
76A	Southern Tech, Marietta
76B	Commencement exercises, Kennesaw State College, Kennesaw
77	College students
78, 79	Soccer game, East Cobb Metro Field
79	Tom Keene
80, 81	Overlook Building, Vinings
82	Greg Wood, Arch-I-Tech Doors, East Cobb Small Business Person 1989
82, 83	Corporate office interior
84	Corporate office interior
85	Cobb commuters on expressway to Atlanta
86, 87	Marietta construction worker
87	Brumby Rocker Factory, Marietta
88	Great American Scream Machine, Six Flags Over Georgia
89	John Wynn, Acadia Coffee Service, Young Entrepreneur Nominee, 1990
90, 91	C-5 transport, Lockheed Aeronautical Systems Company, Marietta
92	Headquarters, Cobb Chamber of Commerce, Marietta
92, 93	Lobby, Stouffer-Waverly Hotel, The Galleria, Smyrna
94	Barrett office interior, Kennesaw
94, 95	White Water, Marietta
95	Brenda Roberts Branch
122, 123	Log Cabin Church, Vinings
124	La Petit Acrobats, Worldfest 1990
125	Worldfest 1990
126	Civil War Reenactment, Kennesaw Mountain National Battlefield Park, Kennesaw
127	Bill of Rights exhibit, Cobb Civic Center, Marietta
128, 129	Sally Danner and Billy Payne, Beaux Arts Ball, The Galleria, Smyrna
129A	*Elizabeth the Queen,* Theatre in the Square, Marietta
129B	*Zion!,* Theatre in the Square, Marietta
130, 131	Dancers prepare for Georgia Ballet's production of *Giselle*
131	*Giselle,* Georgia Ballet, Marietta
132, 133	Cobb Symphony Orchestra
134, 135	Cecy Guerry, Marietta/Cobb Museum of Art, Marietta
136	Quilt Show, Cobb Civic Center, Marietta
137	Chic Lotts, Jubilee Arts Festival
138, 139	Lillie Glass Blowers, Smyrna
140	Summit of Kennesaw Mountain, Kennesaw
140, 141	Little League game, Marietta
142	Little League game, Marietta
143	Porter Wagoner, North Georgia Fair
144, 145	Worldfest 1990
145A	Worldfest 1990
145B	Worldfest 1990
146	Soccer game, East Cobb Metro Field
147	Tennis courts, Powder Springs
148	Sope Creek Paper Mill Ruins
148, 149	BellSouth Atlanta Golf Classic 1991
150	Canadian goose, Austell
151	Sun Valley, Powder Springs
152	Space Shuttle, Six Flags Over Georgia
153	July 4th on the Chattahoochee River
154, 155	Mt. Bethel Methodist Church, Marietta (small)
154, 155	Marietta First Baptist Church, St. James Episcopal Church, Marietta (large)
156, 157	Rabbi Shalom Lewis, Congregation Etz Chaim
157	Camille Sessions Hegg
158, 159	Christmas morning 1990, Marietta
160, 161	Shillings on the Square, Marietta
161	Town Center Mall, Kennesaw
162	Dempsey and Connie Kirk, Jubilee Arts Festival
163	Symphony performance, Jubilee Arts Festival
168	North Georgia Fair
Back end	Fulton-Cobb ferry across Chattahoochee River (circa 1900)

INDEX